marie claire

summer

SIMPLY FRESH FOOD

Michele Cranston

MURDOCH BOOKS

marie claire
summer

contents

Simple fresh food

Summer is all about easy, great tasting and healthy food with a sense of adventure and fun. With this in mind, I thought it might be nice for this book to indulge in a little escapism. While I admit that this was somewhat of a selfish desire on my behalf to run away from the daily madness of a busy life filled with children and work, I suspect that I am not the only one who daydreams about sitting under a swaying palm tree.

I don't know what it is about sandy beaches and blue seas but when most of us think of escaping there's often a desert island thrown into the plan somewhere along the way. Is it the mesmerizing heat, the perfect emptiness of a watery horizon or just that calming sense of being away? Whatever the attraction, when we think of indulgent relaxation we tend to think of locations such as these. And when I start to think of such places my mind turns to food ... of course!

Think of the joy that comes from sharing good times and great food with friends and family. Great food isn't difficult or time consuming to prepare, and it doesn't have to make a statement. It can be as simple as fresh vegetables ready for poaching or serving with savoury dips; as old fashioned as a family roast, as modern as flavoursome crumbs sprinkled over a leafy salad, as sweet as afternoon tea or as heart warming as a winter stew. In other words, I mean real food, simply cooked.

By great food, I mean honest food—fresh and full of flavour with very little fuss involved; easily prepared from good quality seasonal ingredients. While you might not always have access to organic food, there is intrinsic value in knowing where your food has come from, how fresh it is and how it has been grown. Visit a growers' market—see what is locally grown or made, and be inspired.

In warm weather, crunch on leafy salads, sizzling meals from the barbecue or crisp healthy bowls of nature's goodness. In the colder months, prepare slow-cooked meals that have been simmered in a pot or roasted in the oven. Whatever the season, great food is all about enjoying the real and relishing the simple.

Luscious tropical fruit, leafy bowls of salad, grilled seafood, tangy Asian noodles and spiced couscous … food that not only tastes great but is good for you. Food that is bursting with colour, dripping with yummy juices and spiced with a splash of lime, a scattering of herbs and a sprinkle of seasoning. While most of us can't sit in a crystal sea eating juicy ripe mangoes with salty hands we can sit down to a beautiful salad of fresh papaya and briny prosciutto. And that is the wonderful thing about food — that it can, in a simple mouthful, take us to another place.

So let's all lose ourselves on an idyllic island somewhere in the middle of a perfect sea … even if only for an hour or two. And don't panic about the task ahead — while I may have become lost in the thrall of ingredients and flavours, I've kept my feet planted firmly in the sand.

The recipes are easy and use simple ingredients, so you too can relax and enjoy the journey.

fruit

sunny days tantalising flavours tangy bite sweetness and light

NUTTY BANANA BREAD ▪ PINEAPPLE SALAD
BLACK STICKY RICE WITH FRESH PAPAYA
TROPICAL FRUIT WITH ROSEWATER SYRUP
SUMMER NECTARINE 'JAM' ▪ COCONUT MUESLI
SPINACH AND COCONUT SOUP ▪ GREEN PAPAYA AND CHICKEN SALAD
CHILLED TOMATO SOUP ▪ GREEN MANGO SALAD
PROSCIUTTO AND MANGO SALAD ▪ ROAST PORK WITH A PINEAPPLE GLAZE
CHICKEN AND PEPPERED PEACH SALAD ▪ ORANGE AND WATERCRESS SALAD
CHICKEN WITH COCONUT SAMBAL ▪ WATERMELON AND FETA SALAD
DUCK CURRY WITH LYCHEES ▪ ROASTED DUCK BREAST SALAD
CHICKEN SALAD WITH FRESH COCONUT
ROAST PORK WITH MANGO CHUTNEY
MACERATED PLUMS WITH COCONUT SORBET
VERY VANILLA PEACH MERINGUES
RUM AND PINEAPPLE ICE ▪ ROSY PLUM CRUMBLES
WARM PEACHES WITH CINNAMON CREAM
LEMON GRASS GRANITA ▪ PEACHY FRUIT SALAD
HONEY-SPICED PARFAIT WITH FRESH BERRIES
PASSIONFRUIT JELLY WITH FRESH MANGO

nutty banana bread

90 g (3¼ oz) butter
2 eggs
175 g (6 oz/½ cup) golden syrup or honey
250 g (9 oz/2 cups) plain (all-purpose) flour
2 teaspoons baking powder
½ teaspoon bicarbonate of soda (baking soda)
2 large ripe bananas
100 g (3½ oz/1 cup) pecans, roughly chopped
2 tablespoons poppy seeds
1 tablespoon grated lemon zest
butter, extra, to serve
sliced mango, to serve
plain or Greek-style yoghurt, to serve

Preheat the oven to 180°C (350°F/Gas 4). Lightly grease an 8 x 22 cm (3¼ x 8½ inch) loaf (bar) tin and line it with baking paper.

Put the butter, eggs, golden syrup, flour, baking powder, bicarbonate of soda and bananas in a food processor and blend to a smooth dough. Add the pecans, poppy seeds and lemon zest and pulse until just combined.

Pour the mixture into the loaf tin and bake for 40 minutes, or until a skewer inserted into the centre of the loaf comes away clean. Allow to cool in the tin before slicing. Serve warm, generously spread with butter, or toasted with sliced mango and a dollop of yoghurt.

MAKES 10 SLICES

pineapple salad

1 pineapple
8 mint leaves, finely sliced
2 tablespoons lime juice
½ teaspoon caster (superfine) sugar
1 teaspoon orange flower water
3 tablespoons passionfruit pulp

Slice the skin off the pineapple, cutting out any brown 'eyes'. Cut the pineapple into quarters lengthways and remove the woody core. Finely slice the trimmed quarters into bite-sized pieces and put them in a bowl with the mint.

In a small bowl, mix together the lime juice, sugar, orange flower water and passionfruit pulp. Pour the mixture over the pineapple and lightly toss to combine.

SERVES 4

black sticky rice with fresh papaya

200 g (7 oz/1 cup) black rice
4 tablespoons grated palm sugar or soft
   brown sugar
1 teaspoon natural vanilla extract
125 ml (4 fl oz/½ cup) coconut milk
fresh papaya or banana slices, to serve
coconut milk, extra, for drizzling

Soak the rice in plenty of cold water for 1 hour. Drain, rinse, then drain again. Put the rice in a saucepan with 500 ml (17 fl oz/2 cups) of water. Bring to the boil, stirring occasionally, then reduce the heat to low. Cover and simmer for 35 minutes.

Stir through the sugar, vanilla extract, coconut milk and a pinch of salt. Simmer over low heat, uncovered, for a further 10 minutes, then take the rice off the heat and allow to cool. Serve with slices of fresh papaya or banana and a drizzle of coconut milk.

SERVES 4

tropical fruit with rosewater syrup

3 tablespoons sugar
2 tablespoons lime juice
¼ teaspoon rosewater
1 large mango, peeled, seeded and diced
1 large red papaya, peeled, seeded and diced
12 fresh lychees, peeled, or 400 g (14 oz) tinned
lychees, drained
shaved coconut (Basics), to serve

To make the rosewater syrup, put the sugar in a small saucepan with 125 ml (4 fl oz/½ cup) of water and bring to the boil. Reduce the heat and simmer for 5 minutes, stirring occasionally to ensure that the sugar melts completely. Take the pan off the heat and allow to cool completely. Stir in the lime juice and rosewater, then pour the syrup into a small glass bowl and chill in the refrigerator until ready to use.

Divide all the fruit among four bowls, scatter with slivers of shaved coconut and drizzle with some of the syrup.

SERVES 4

summer nectarine 'jam'

4 large nectarines (about 600 g/1 lb 5 oz in total)
4 tablespoons sugar
½ vanilla bean, split
½ teaspoon orange flower water
8 slices nutty banana bread (page 14) or walnut bread (Basics),
toasted and buttered

Remove the stones from the nectarines, then thickly slice the flesh
and put the slices in a saucepan. Add the sugar, vanilla bean and
4 tablespoons of water. Simmer over low heat for 18–20 minutes, or
until the nectarines are just beginning to break up.

Remove the vanilla bean and add the orange flower water. Serve
spooned over slices of toasted and buttered banana or walnut bread.

SERVES 4–6

coconut muesli

400 g (14 oz/4 cups) rolled
   (porridge) oats
125 g (4½ oz/1 cup) unsalted
   sunflower seeds
2 tablespoons sesame seeds
125 g (4½ oz/1 cup) slivered almonds
120 g (4¼ oz/2 cups) shredded coconut
250 ml (9 fl oz oz/¾ cup) maple syrup
4 tablespoons vegetable oil
40 g (1½ oz/¼ cup) finely sliced
   dried peaches
35 g (1¼ oz/¼ cup) finely sliced
   dried mango

Preheat the oven to 150°C (300°F/Gas 2).
Put the oats in a large bowl with the
sunflower seeds, sesame seeds, almonds
and coconut and mix well.

Heat the maple syrup and oil in a small
saucepan over low heat. Pour the warm
mixture over the muesli and stir so that all
the grains and seeds are well covered.

Spread the mixture over two baking trays
and bake for 30 minutes, stirring
occasionally, and swapping the trays
around in the oven halfway through baking.
Remove from the oven and allow to cool.

Transfer to a large bowl, add the peach and
mango and toss well. The muesli can be
stored in an airtight container for up to
1 month. Makes about 1.2 kg (2 lb 10 oz).

SERVES 12

spinach and coconut soup

2 bunches English spinach (about
    1 kg/2 lb 4 oz in total)
4 tablespoons olive oil
2 onions, finely sliced
2 garlic cloves, finely chopped
½ teaspoon ground cumin
500 ml (17 fl oz/2 cups) vegetable stock
400 ml (14 fl oz) tin coconut milk

Rinse the spinach under cold running water, then drain and roughly chop. Heat the olive oil in a large saucepan over medium heat. Add the onion, garlic and cumin and sauté for 5 minutes, or until the onion is soft and translucent.

Add the spinach, cover and cook for 2–3 minutes, then toss the spinach about a little so that it cooks evenly. When all the spinach has sweated down to a dark green colour, take the pan off the heat.

Put the spinach in a blender with half the stock. Blend until smooth, then return to the saucepan. Stir in the coconut milk and remaining stock and warm the soup over medium heat. Season to taste with sea salt and ground white pepper.

SERVES 6

green papaya and chicken salad

1 lemon grass stem, trimmed
juice of 1 lemon
1 tablespoon sea salt
2 boneless, skinless chicken breasts
2 tablespoons tamarind purée
1 teaspoon soy sauce
2 teaspoons finely grated fresh ginger
1 tablespoon grated palm sugar or soft brown sugar
½ teaspoon ground cumin
1 large red chilli, seeded and finely sliced
3 spring onions (scallions), finely sliced
1 large green papaya (about 650 g/1 lb 7 oz), peeled
    and seeded, flesh shredded
1 handful mint
1 handful coriander (cilantro) leaves

Put a large pot of water over high heat and bring to the boil. Cut the
lemon grass stem into several pieces and add them to the pot along
with the lemon juice and salt. When the water has begun to boil, add
the chicken breasts, then cover the pot and take it off the heat for
40 minutes — during this time the residual heat will gently poach the
chicken. Lift the chicken out of the liquid and allow to cool before
shredding the meat.

Put the tamarind purée in a large non-metallic bowl and add 125 ml
(4 fl oz/½ cup) of water. Stir to combine, then add the soy sauce,
ginger, sugar, cumin and chilli. Stir until the sugar has dissolved.

Add the shredded chicken, spring onion, papaya, mint and coriander
and toss to combine.

SERVES 4

chilled tomato soup

2 teaspoons sea salt
1 teaspoon ground cumin
½ teaspoon ground white pepper
1 tablespoon finely grated fresh ginger
2 tablespoons olive oil
10 large vine-ripened tomatoes
10 mint leaves
125 ml (4 fl oz/½ cup) dry sherry
small mint leaves, extra, to serve

Preheat the oven to 180°C (350°F/Gas 4). In a small bowl, combine the sea salt, cumin, white pepper, ginger and olive oil.

Using a small, sharp-pointed knife, remove the stem of one tomato with a circular action to make a crater in the top. Repeat with the other tomatoes and sit them on a baking tray. Fill the top of each tomato with the salt mixture, then bake for 30 minutes, or until they are soft and starting to split. Remove from the oven and allow to cool.

Roughly chop the tomatoes, then put them in a blender or food processor along with the mint. Blend to a purée, strain into a large bowl, then stir in the sherry. Cover with plastic wrap and chill until ready to serve. Spoon into four bowls and add a scattering of small mint leaves.

SERVES 4

green mango salad

6 mint leaves
1½ tablespoons lime juice
1½ tablespoons fish sauce
1 tablespoon caster (superfine) sugar
1 small red chilli, seeded and finely
   chopped
3 green mangoes
2 tablespoons finely chopped roasted
   peanuts
1 handful coriander (cilantro) leaves
small cos (romaine) lettuce leaves or
   betel leaves, to serve (optional)

Finely chop the mint leaves and put them in a large non-metallic bowl with the lime juice, fish sauce, sugar and chilli. Stir until the sugar has dissolved, then set the dressing aside.

Peel the mangoes and cut the flesh away from the seed. Finely julienne or grate the flesh and add it to the dressing, along with the peanuts, coriander leaves and remaining mint. Toss to combine and serve the salad as a side dish, or on small cos lettuce or betel leaves as a refreshing starter.

SERVES 4

prosciutto and mango salad

1½ tablespoons olive oil
2 teaspoons red wine vinegar
6 kalamata olives, pitted and roughly chopped
1 teaspoon thyme leaves
100 g (3½ oz/2¾ cups) mizuna or baby salad leaves
2 mangoes, peeled, seeded and diced
4 slices prosciutto
40 g (1½ oz/⅓ cup) slivered almonds, toasted

Put the olive oil, vinegar, olives and thyme in a small bowl and lightly season with sea salt and freshly ground black pepper. Mix together to make a dressing and set aside.

Put the salad leaves on a serving platter, then arrange the mango over the top. Roughly tear the prosciutto into bite-sized pieces and scatter over the salad.

Stir the dressing again, then drizzle it over the salad before scattering with the almonds.

SERVES 4

roast pork with a pineapple glaze

500 ml (17 fl oz/2 cups) pineapple juice
3 tablespoons maple syrup
2 garlic cloves, finely chopped
4 star anise
2 cinnamon sticks
3 large red chillies, seeded and cut into large pieces
1 kg (2 lb 4 oz) pork loin, skin cut off and reserved
2 tablespoons balsamic vinegar
12 thin pineapple slices, skin and core removed
green salad, to serve

Make a marinade by mixing the pineapple juice and maple syrup together in a large bowl with the garlic, star anise, cinnamon sticks and chilli. Using a sharp knife, cut 5 mm (¼ inch) deep slashes, 4–5 cm (1½–2 inches) apart, into the pork. Sit the pork in the marinade, roll it around until well coated, then cover and marinate in the refrigerator overnight.

Heat the oven to 200°C (400°F/Gas 6). Lift the pork into a roasting tin, pour the marinade all over and around the pork, then cover with foil and roast for 40 minutes.

Meanwhile, make the crackling. Score the pork skin lightly with a very sharp knife, then cut it into several strips. Put the strips in a roasting tin, brush them with water, sprinkle with salt and roast for 20 minutes, or until golden brown and crackly. Drain off any fat.

Take the foil off the pork and baste the meat with the pan juices. Roast, uncovered, for a further 30–35 minutes, or until the juices run clear when a skewer is inserted into the thickest part of the meat. Loosely cover the pork with foil and allow to rest for 10 minutes. Meanwhile, stir the vinegar into the pan juices.

Carve the pork and serve on the pineapple slices with a spoonful of pan juices, a green salad and some bits of crackling.

SERVES 6

chicken and peppered peach salad

1½ tablespoons white wine vinegar
125 ml (4 fl oz/½ cup) olive oil
1½ teaspoons freshly ground
    black pepper
4 ripe peaches
100 g (3½ oz/2¼ cups) baby English
    spinach leaves
200 g (7 oz/2 cups) shredded
    roast chicken

In a large bowl, combine the white wine vinegar, olive oil and ground black pepper. Slice the peaches into the pepper dressing and lightly toss to coat.

Arrange the spinach leaves on a serving platter or in a bowl. Add the dressed peaches and the shredded chicken and season with a little sea salt.

SERVES 4

orange and watercress salad

½ red onion, very finely sliced
1 teaspoon sea salt
4 oranges
2 handfuls of picked watercress sprigs
20 niçoise olives
1 tablespoon red wine vinegar
2 tablespoons extra virgin olive oil

Put the onion in a sieve over a bowl and sprinkle with the sea salt.

Using a sharp knife, cut the top and bottom off the oranges. Stand the oranges on a chopping board and slice away the skin and pith. Working over a large bowl to catch the juices, remove the segments by running a knife between each membrane. Put the segments in the bowl with the captured orange juice, the watercress sprigs and the olives. Mix well.

Rinse the onion slices, then press between paper towels to squeeze out any excess liquid. Put them in a small bowl and pour over the red wine vinegar.

Arrange the orange salad on a serving platter, then scatter over the vinegary onion and drizzle with olive oil.

SERVES 4

chicken with coconut sambal

2 teaspoons vegetable oil
1 tablespoon finely chopped lemon grass (white part only)
1 seeded and finely chopped large red chilli
½ finely diced onion
3 tablespoons desiccated coconut
1 teaspoon dark brown sugar
½ teaspoon sea salt
2 poached boneless, skinless chicken breasts
3 tablespoons olive oil
1 tablespoon lime juice
100 g (3½ oz/2¼ cups) baby English spinach leaves
1 sliced large red papaya

To make the coconut sambal, heat the vegetable oil in a frying pan over medium heat. Add the lemon grass, chilli and onion. Cook, stirring, for 5 minutes. Reduce the heat to low and stir in the coconut, brown sugar and sea salt. Cook, stirring, for 5 minutes, or until golden and crisp.

Take off the heat and allow to cool. Shred the chicken breasts, put them in a bowl and mix through olive oil and the lime juice. Pile the spinach leaves on a serving platter. Arrange the papaya over the top, add the chicken and sprinkle with the coconut sambal.

SERVES 4

watermelon and feta salad

750 g (1 lb 10 oz) portion of seedless
    watermelon
200 g (7 oz) Bulgarian feta cheese, cut
    into 2 cm (¾ inch) cubes
20 kalamata olives, pitted and sliced
12 mint leaves, finely sliced
2 celery stalks, finely diced
1 tablespoon red wine vinegar
2 tablespoons olive oil

Take the watermelon, cut away the rind,
then cut the flesh into bite-sized chunks.
Roughly pile the feta and watermelon onto
a serving platter, then scatter the olives,
mint leaves and celery over the top.

Mix together red wine vinegar and olive oil
and pour over the salad. Season with
freshly ground black pepper.

SERVES 4

duck curry with lychees

1 whole duck, rinsed and dried
1 onion, finely diced
2 garlic cloves, crushed
1 tablespoon finely grated fresh ginger
1 teaspoon chilli powder
2 tablespoons finely chopped lemon grass,
   white part only
½ teaspoon ground turmeric
2 tablespoons tamarind purée
400 ml (14 fl oz) tin coconut milk
4 makrut (kaffir lime) leaves
12 fresh lychees, peeled, or 400 g (14 oz)
   tinned lychees, drained
steamed white rice (Basics), to serve

Using a cleaver or heavy, sharp knife, cut the duck into 8–10 pieces, through the joints and across the breast (you could ask your butcher to do this, if you prefer). Put a wok or large saucepan over high heat and sear the duck pieces in two batches for 2–3 minutes each time, or until the skin is crispy and golden. Remove to a plate.

Reduce the heat to low and add the onion, garlic, ginger, chilli powder, lemon grass and turmeric to the wok or pan. Fry for 2 minutes, or until the onion is soft, then add the tamarind purée, coconut milk, lime leaves and 250 ml (9 fl oz/1 cup) of water. Simmer for 5 minutes.

Add the duck and simmer for 40 minutes, then add the lychees and cook for a further 5 minutes to heat through. Serve with steamed white rice.

SERVES 4

roasted duck breast salad

2 tablespoons dark brown sugar
¼ teaspoon Chinese five-spice
1 teaspoon sea salt
4 boneless duck breasts, skin on
½ teaspoon sichuan peppercorns
100 g (3½ oz/2¾ cups) mizuna, mesclun
    or baby salad leaves
2 mangoes, peeled, seeded and sliced
2 spring onions (scallions), finely sliced
    on the diagonal
2 tablespoons Chinese black vinegar

Preheat the oven to 180°C (350°F/Gas 4). In a small bowl, combine the
sugar, five-spice and sea salt. Using a sharp knife, lightly score the
skin of the duck breasts in a crisscross pattern, then rub the sugar
mixture into the duck skin.

Heat a non-stick frying pan over high heat and sear the duck breasts,
skin side down, for a few minutes, or until crisp — the skin will go
quite dark as the sugar caramelizes. Put the duck breasts, skin side
up, on a rack set over a baking tray and roast for 15 minutes. Remove
the tray from the oven, cover with foil and allow the duck to rest for
a few minutes.

Roughly grind the peppercorns using a mortar and pestle. Arrange the
salad leaves, mango and spring onion on four serving plates. Finely
slice the duck breasts diagonally across the grain and arrange over
the salad. Drizzle the duck with the Chinese black vinegar and
sprinkle with the ground peppercorns.

SERVES 4

chicken salad with fresh coconut

2 tablespoons finely chopped lemon grass
   (white part only)
1 teaspoon grated palm sugar (or soft brown sugar)
200 ml (7 fl oz) coconut milk
3 tablespoons lime juice
1 teaspoon sesame oil
2 boneless, skinless chicken breasts
1 handful mint
¼ fresh coconut, flesh shaved (Basics)
100 g (3½ oz) snow pea (mangetout) shoots
2 Lebanese (short) cucumbers, finely sliced
2 tablespoons sesame seeds, toasted
lime wedges, to serve

Preheat the oven to 180°C (350°F/Gas 4). Make a dressing by putting the lemon grass, sugar, coconut milk and 2 tablespoons of the lime juice in a saucepan over low heat. Simmer for 5 minutes, stirring occasionally to ensure the sugar dissolves, then take the pan off the heat and allow the dressing to cool.

Put the sesame oil and remaining lime juice in a small baking dish. Add the chicken breasts and toss well to coat, then cover with foil and bake for 30 minutes. Remove the chicken from the oven and let it cool completely, keeping the baking dish covered.

Roughly shred the chicken and stir it through the dressing. Add the mint, coconut, snow pea shoots, cucumber and sesame seeds and toss together well. Serve with lime wedges.

SERVES 4

roast pork with mango chutney

1 tablespoon olive oil
1 red onion, finely diced
1 tablespoon finely grated fresh ginger
2 tablespoons finely chopped lemon grass,
     white part only
2 tablespoons tamarind purée
125 ml (4 fl oz/½ cup) white wine vinegar
115 g (4 oz/½ cup) dark brown sugar
1 large red chilli, seeded and finely chopped
2 just-ripe mangoes, peeled, seeded and diced
1.5 kg (3 lb 5 oz) pork shoulder, skin scored
     (ask your butcher to do this)
green salad, to serve

To make the mango chutney, heat the olive oil in a saucepan over medium heat and add the onion, ginger and lemon grass. Cook, stirring, for 10–12 minutes, or until the onion is slightly caramelized. Stir in the tamarind purée, vinegar, sugar, chilli and mango.

Bring to the boil, then reduce the heat and simmer for 20 minutes. Set aside.

Meanwhile, preheat the oven to 220°C (425°F/Gas 7). Pat the pork dry with paper towels and rub the scored skin well with salt. Season with freshly ground black pepper. Sit the pork in a roasting tin, skin side up, and roast for 25 minutes, then turn the oven temperature down to 180°C (350°F/Gas 4) and cook for a further 1 hour. To test if the meat is done, insert a sharp knife or skewer into the centre — the juices should run clear.

Transfer the pork to a warm serving platter, cover with foil and leave to rest for 15 minutes. If the skin isn't quite crunchy and needs further cooking, slice it off using a sharp knife, put it back in the roasting tin and roast on the top shelf of the oven for a few minutes. Carve the pork and serve with the mango chutney and a green salad.

SERVES 6

macerated plums with coconut sorbet

145 g (5 oz/²/₃ cup) caster (superfine) sugar
1 vanilla bean
250 ml (9 fl oz/1 cup) milk
400 ml (14 fl oz) tin coconut milk
1 tablespoon golden rum
10 blood plums (about 800 g/1 lb 12 oz in total)
2 tablespoons dark brown sugar
juice of 1 orange

Put the caster sugar, vanilla bean and 150 ml (5 fl oz) of water
in a saucepan over medium heat. Stir well to dissolve the sugar.
When the syrup comes to the boil, let it bubble for 10 minutes.
Discard the vanilla bean and pour the syrup into a bowl.

To make the coconut sorbet, pour the milk and coconut milk into the
saucepan and let it warm through. Take the pan off the heat, stir in
the vanilla syrup and rum, then allow to cool. Churn the mixture in an
ice cream machine, or pour it into a shallow container, place it in the
freezer, then stir every hour until the sorbet freezes.

Cut the plums into thick slices, removing the stones as you go. Put
the plums in a bowl, add the dark brown sugar and orange juice and
toss until well coated. Cover and refrigerate for 1 hour. Divide the
chilled plums among six bowls and serve with the coconut sorbet.

SERVES 6

very vanilla peach meringues

4 egg whites
230 g (8 oz/1 cup) caster (superfine) sugar
2 vanilla beans
½ teaspoon natural vanilla extract
6 peaches, stones removed, cut in half
250 ml (9 fl oz/1 cup) dessert wine
3 tablespoons raw caster (superfine) sugar
300 ml (10½ fl oz) crème fraîche or thick (double/heavy) cream

Preheat the oven to 110°C (225°F/Gas ½). Line two large baking trays with baking paper.

Whisk the egg whites until stiff but not dry. Gradually whisk in half the caster sugar, whisking until very shiny, then add the remaining caster sugar and lightly whisk until incorporated. Split a vanilla bean along its length, scrape out the seeds with the tip of a knife and stir them into the egg whites, along with the vanilla extract.

Spoon the mixture onto the baking trays to form six 10–12 cm (4–4½ inch) rounds. Bake for 1½ hours, or until crisp and golden. Turn the oven off, open the door slightly and leave the meringues to cool. When cool enough to handle, peel the meringues off the baking paper and put them on a rack to cool.

Turn the oven temperature up to 210°C (415°F/Gas 6–7). Put the peaches, cut side up, in a single layer in a baking dish. Pour the wine over the top and sprinkle with the raw sugar. Split the remaining vanilla bean in half, cut it into thirds and add to the baking dish. Bake for 15 minutes, or until the peaches are soft and slightly caramelized on top. Remove from the oven and allow to cool.

Divide the meringues among six serving plates and top with a dollop of crème fraîche or cream. Add two peach halves to each plate and drizzle with the syrup from the baking dish. Garnish with the vanilla bean pieces.

SERVES 6

rum and pineapple ice

55 g (2 oz/¼ cup) caster
    (superfine) sugar
500 ml (17 fl oz/2 cups)
    pineapple juice
100 ml (3½ fl oz) golden rum
1 teaspoon natural vanilla extract
2 tablespoons coconut milk

Put the caster sugar and the pineapple
juice in a saucepan over medium heat. Stir
until the sugar has dissolved, then remove
from the heat and stir in the rum and
vanilla extract.

Pour the liquid into a wide shallow
container and freeze for 4–5 hours, or until
frozen. Remove from the freezer and allow
to soften, then break the mixture up using
a fork until it looks like crushed ice. Return
to the freezer until ready to serve.

Spoon into four chilled parfait glasses and
drizzle each with coconut milk.

SERVES 4

rosy plum crumbles

10 blood plums (about 800 g/
   1 lb 12 oz in total)
80 g (2¾ oz/⅓ cup) caster
   (superfine) sugar
1 teaspoon rosewater
115 g (4 oz/½ cup) dark brown sugar
60 g (2¼ oz/½ cup) plain
   (all-purpose) flour
45 g (1½ oz/½ cup) desiccated coconut
75 g (2½ oz) unsalted butter
whipped cream or thick (double/heavy)
   cream, to serve

Preheat the oven to 180°C (350°F/Gas 4).
Slice the plums, removing the stones, and
put them in a bowl. Add the caster sugar
and rosewater and toss until the plums are
well coated in sugar. Set aside for 10 minutes.

Toss the brown sugar, flour and coconut
together in a bowl. Rub the butter in with
your fingertips until the mixture resembles
breadcrumbs. Set aside.

Stir the plums to ensure they are well coated,
divide among six 150 ml (5 fl oz) ovenproof
bowls, piling the plums above the top of the
bowls as they will cook down quite a bit.

Top the plums with the coconut mixture,
then sit the bowls on a baking tray and bake
for 30 minutes, or until the crumbles are
golden and the juices are bubbling over the
sides of the bowls. Serve warm with cream.

SERVES 6

warm peaches with cinnamon cream

3 tablespoons plain yoghurt
¼ teaspoon ground cinnamon
½ teaspoon natural vanilla extract
1 teaspoon caster (superfine) sugar
150 ml (5 fl oz) whipped cream
4 ripe peaches
4 tablespoons raw caster (superfine) sugar, or
light brown sugar
pistachio biscotti (Basics), cardamom almond bread (Basics)
or sweet wafers, to serve

To make the cinnamon cream, put the plain yoghurt in a bowl with
the cinnamon, vanilla extract and caster sugar. Stir until the sugar has
dissolved. Fold through the whipped cream, then cover with plastic
wrap and chill until ready to serve.

Cut the peaches in half and remove the stones. Sit the peaches on a
tray, cut side up, and sprinkle with the raw caster. Cook under a hot
grill (broiler) for 10 minutes, or until the sugar is beginning to darken.
Serve with the cinnamon cream and some pistachio biscotti,
cardamom almond bread or sweet wafers.

SERVES 4

lemon grass granita

2 lemon grass stems, trimmed
145 g (5¼ oz/⅔ cup) caster (superfine) sugar
500 ml (17 fl oz/2 cups) water
250 ml (9 fl oz/1 cup) pineapple juice
2 limes, juiced
100 ml (3½ fl oz) vodka
½ small, ripe pineapple, cut into thin wedges

Cut the lemon grass stems into thirds and bruise them with the handle of a heavy knife. Put them in a saucepan with the sugar and water. Bring to the boil, reduce the heat and simmer for 5 minutes. Take off the heat and allow to cool.

Stir in the pineapple juice, lime juice and vodka. Strain into a wide, shallow container and freeze for 1 hour. Using a fork, scrape the ice from the edges back into the liquid. Return to the freezer and repeat another three times, until the granita looks like crushed ice. Divide the sliced pineapple among serving plates. Serve the granita on the side, in chilled glasses.

SERVES 4–6

peachy fruit salad

4 peaches, cut in half
2 bananas, sliced
4 passionfruit
2 oranges, juiced
1 tablespoon caster (superfine) sugar
ice cream, sorbet or creamy yoghurt, to serve

Remove the stones and skins from the peaches. Slice the peaches into a bowl. Add the bananas and the pulp of the passionfruit. Cover with the orange juice and sprinkle with the sugar. Lightly stir to just coat the fruit in the sweet juice. Serve with ice cream, sorbet or creamy yoghurt.

SERVES 4

honey-spiced parfait with fresh berries

5 egg yolks
100 g (3½ oz) caster (superfine) sugar
2 tablespoons honey
¼ teaspoon ground cardamom
500 ml (17 fl oz/2 cups) crème fraîche
    or sour cream
fresh berries, such as raspberries,
    blackberries or strawberries,
    to serve

Using a whisk or electric beaters, whisk the egg yolks, sugar and honey in a large bowl until thick and pale.

Gently fold the cardamom and crème fraîche through, then spoon into an 8 x 22 cm (3¼ x 8½ inch) loaf (bar) tin lined with baking paper. Freeze overnight, or until firm.

Cut the parfait into six thick slices and serve with fresh berries.

SERVES 6

passionfruit jelly with fresh mango

8–10 passionfruit, pulp removed
300 ml (10½ fl oz) pineapple juice
140 g (5 oz/⅔ cup) sugar
2 tablespoons lime juice
6 gelatine leaves
2 ripe mangoes
cream (whipping), to serve

Put the passionfruit pulp into a sieve over a bowl. Using a spoon, work the seeds into the sieve to extract as much juice as possible — you will need 60 ml (2 fl oz/ ¼ cup) of passionfruit juice for the jelly.

Put the pineapple juice and sugar in a saucepan with 200 ml (7 fl oz) of water and stir over medium heat until the sugar has dissolved. Remove from the heat and stir in the passionfruit and lime juices. Pour 600 ml (21 fl oz) of the liquid into a measuring cup.

Fill a bowl with cold water and soak the gelatine for a few minutes until dissolved to a jellied consistency. Squeeze excess water from gelatine and add to the juice mixture. Stir to completely dissolve the gelatine. Pour into a bowl, cover with plastic wrap and refrigerate for several hours until firm.

Remove the skin and stones from mangoes and roughly chop the flesh into bite-sized pieces. Layer spoonfuls of the jelly and mango in six chilled glasses. Serve with cream.

SERVES 6

leaf

leafy greens, bowls of goodness
herbs and citrus, flavour and crunch

SMOKED SALMON WITH VEGETABLE SALAD ▪ LABNEH SALAD

AROMATIC ROAST CHICKEN BREASTS ▪ BOCCONCINI SALAD

SPINACH AND CHICKPEA SALAD ▪ CHILLED CUCUMBER SOUP

ROAST DUCK AND SWEET POTATO SALAD

FRAGRANT LIME AND LEMON GRASS CHICKEN

SEARED LAMB WITH ALMOND SALAD

LAMB SALAD WITH WALNUT PESTO

SESAME DUCK SALAD ▪ SESAME GREENS

CRAB AND GREEN BEAN SALAD ▪ PUMPKIN AND HAZELNUT SALAD

CAPSICUM RELISH ON BABY COS ▪ LENTIL AND BEETROOT SALAD

CHICKEN AND PINE NUT SALAD ▪ TUNA SALAD IN LETTUCE CUPS

MA HOR ON BETEL LEAVES ▪ SAN CHOY BAU

SALMON WRAPPED IN VINE LEAVES ▪ ROAST PUMPKIN AND TOFU SALAD

FRIED SHALLOT AND CASHEW SALAD

ROCKET AND PEAR SALAD

LAMB SKEWERS WITH HERBED YOGHURT ▪ FRIED TOFU SALAD

TOFU, BROCCOLINI AND ALMONDS

smoked salmon with vegetable salad

1 fennel bulb
2 zucchini (courgettes)
2 Lebanese (short) cucumbers
1 teaspoon finely chopped mint
1 teaspoon finely chopped dill
1 tablespoon olive oil
2 tablespoons lemon juice
1 teaspoon caster (superfine) sugar
½ teaspoon sea salt
16 slices smoked salmon

Trim the base of the fennel, slice the bulb as finely as possible and put it in a bowl. Slice the zucchini and cucumbers as finely as possible, cutting them on the diagonal, and add them to the fennel. Add the mint, dill, olive oil, lemon juice, sugar and sea salt. Toss to combine, then set aside for 10 minutes.

Divide the smoked salmon slices among four plates. Toss the salad one more time before piling it on top of the salmon.

SERVES 4

labneh salad

600 g (1 lb 5 oz) plain yoghurt
1 teaspoon salt
2 garlic cloves, crushed
8 lemon thyme sprigs
extra virgin olive oil, for drizzling
50 g (1¾ oz/¼ cup) burghul (bulgur)
2 tablespoons finely chopped preserved lemon rind
1 handful flat-leaf (Italian) parsley, roughly chopped
100 g (3½ oz/1 heaped cup) flaked almonds, toasted
50 g (1¾ oz/1½ cups) wild rocket (arugula) leaves
toasted pide (Turkish/flat bread), to serve

You can buy labneh in some speciality stores but if you have the time there is something quite satisfying about making your own.

Start by mixing the yoghurt with the salt. Line a sieve with two layers of muslin (cheesecloth) and put it over a bowl. Pour the yoghurt into the sieve, then cover and allow to drain for 2 days in the refrigerator — it should now be very thick and creamy.

Roll the mixture into eight plum-sized balls and sit them in a wide container along with the garlic. Scatter with the thyme sprigs and drizzle with olive oil. Cover and leave to marinate in the refrigerator for 1 more day.

Just before serving time, put the burghul in a bowl and cover with 4 tablespoons of boiling water. Allow to sit for 5 minutes, or until all the water is absorbed. Add the preserved lemon, parsley, almonds and rocket, toss well, then divide among four plates. Top each with two labneh and drizzle with a little more olive oil. Season with sea salt and freshly ground black pepper and serve with toasted pide.

SERVES 4

aromatic roast chicken breasts

1 vanilla bean
2 tablespoons soy sauce
2 tablespoons grated palm sugar
   or soft brown sugar
2 tablespoons grated lemon zest
4 boneless chicken breasts, skin on
juice of 4 lemons
4 tablespoons olive oil
50 g (1¾ oz) snow pea
   (mangetout) shoots
herbed couscous (Basics), to serve

Preheat the oven to 200°C (400°F/Gas 6).
Using a sharp knife, slice the vanilla bean
in half lengthways and scrape the seeds into
a bowl (reserve the vanilla pod for another
use). Add the soy sauce, sugar and lemon
zest and stir to combine.

Using a sharp knife, cut several long incisions
into the skin of each chicken breast, then rub
the soy mixture into the skin. Put the lemon
juice and olive oil in a small casserole dish
or baking dish and add the chicken breasts,
skin side up. Roast for 15 minutes, or until
the chicken is cooked through.

Carve each chicken breast into several thick
slices. Serve with the snow pea shoots on a
bed of herbed couscous, with the baking
juices spooned over the top.

SERVES 4

bocconcini salad

1 tablespoon white wine vinegar
4 tablespoons extra virgin olive oil
20 mint leaves, roughly chopped
1 handful flat-leaf (Italian) parsley, roughly chopped
350 g (12 oz/2 bunches) thin asparagus spears, trimmed
200 g (7 oz) bocconcini (fresh baby mozzarella cheese),
    cut in half
2 avocados

Put the vinegar, olive oil, mint and parsley in a large bowl.

Bring a saucepan of water to the boil. Add the asparagus spears
and blanch for 1 minute, or until they begin to turn emerald green.
Rinse the spears under cold running water, then cut them into 4 cm
(1½ inch) lengths. Add them to the mint and parsley, along with
the bocconcini.

Slice the avocados in half and remove the stones.

Cut the flesh into bite-sized chunks or wedges and add them to the
salad. Season with sea salt and freshly ground black pepper, then
gently toss before serving.

SERVES 4

spinach and chickpea salad

2 bunches English spinach (about 1 kg/
    2 lb 4 oz in total)
2 tablespoons olive oil
1 garlic clove, crushed
400 g (14 oz) tin chickpeas, rinsed and drained
2 tablespoons sumac
1 tablespoon red wine vinegar
4 tablespoons extra virgin olive oil
45 g (1½ oz/½ cup) desiccated coconut, toasted

Trim the spinach and rinse the leaves well under running water. Drain well. Put a heavy-based saucepan over medium heat and add the olive oil and garlic. Finely chop the spinach, add it to the saucepan and cook for a few minutes, just until all the leaves turn a dark emerald green and are softly wilted.

Drain the spinach in a colander to remove any excess liquid, then put it in a large bowl with the chickpeas, sumac, vinegar and olive oil. Toss well to coat the spinach and chickpeas, then add the coconut. Season to taste with sea salt and freshly ground black pepper. Toss again before serving.

SERVES 4–6

chilled cucumber soup

4 Lebanese (short) cucumbers
(about 600 g/1 lb 5 oz in total)
250 g (9 oz/1 cup) plain yoghurt
250 ml (9 fl oz/1 cup) chicken stock
3 tablespoons fine semolina
1 tablespoon lemon juice
1 tablespoon finely chopped dill
4 dill sprigs, extra, to serve

Peel three of the cucumbers, and, if you like, slice the fourth into very thin rounds to garnish the soup.

Roughly chop the peeled cucumbers and put them in a food processor with the yoghurt, stock and semolina. Blend to a smooth soup. Pour into a large pitcher, stir in the lemon juice and chopped dill and season to taste. Cover with plastic wrap and refrigerate for several hours, or until well chilled. If you like, serve garnished with the cucumber rounds and extra dill sprigs.

SERVES 4

roast duck and sweet potato salad

700 g (1 lb 9 oz) orange sweet potatoes
2 tablespoons light olive oil
1 whole Chinese roasted duck
2 tablespoons tamarind purée
1 tablespoon finely grated fresh ginger
2 tablespoons grated palm sugar or soft brown sugar
2 tablespoons lime juice
4 tablespoons olive oil
50 g (1¾ oz/1½ cups) wild rocket (arugula) leaves
50 g (1¾ oz/1½ cups) small tatsoi leaves
3 large red chillies, seeded and finely sliced

Preheat the oven to 180°C (350°F/Gas 4). Peel the sweet potatoes and cut them into bite-sized chunks. Put them on a baking tray and rub with the light olive oil. Season with sea salt and freshly ground black pepper and roast for 30 minutes, or until tender.

Remove the skin from the duck and, using a pair of kitchen scissors, cut it into thin strips. Put the strips on a baking tray and into the hot oven for 10 minutes, or until the skin begins to crisp. Remove and drain on paper towels.

Put the tamarind purée in a large bowl and add 4 tablespoons of water. Add the ginger, sugar, lime juice and olive oil and stir well to make a dressing.

Pull the flesh from the duck and roughly shred it. Add it to the tamarind dressing along with the crispy duck skin and baked sweet potato. Lightly toss, then add the rocket and tatsoi leaves. Pile the salad into six bowls, or arrange over a serving platter, and scatter with the chilli slices.

SERVES 6

fragrant lime and lemon grass chicken

zest and juice of 2 limes
16 cm (6¼ inch) piece of lemon grass, trimmed
    and roughly chopped
2 garlic cloves, peeled
1 tablespoon roughly chopped fresh ginger
2 large red chillies, seeded
1 tablespoon soy sauce
4 boneless, skinless chicken breasts
2 tablespoons olive oil
100 g (3½ oz/2¾ cups) mixed salad leaves
2 handfuls coriander (cilantro) sprigs
2 tablespoons peanuts, toasted and roughly chopped

Preheat the oven to 200°C (400°F/Gas 6). Using a food processor or mortar and pestle, grind the lime zest, lemon grass, garlic, ginger, chilli and soy sauce into a smooth paste.

Rub the paste all over the chicken breasts and sit them in a deep baking tray. Drizzle with the olive oil and lime juice, season with a little sea salt, then cover with foil and bake for 20 minutes. Check that the chicken is cooked through using the pointed end of a sharp knife. Bake a little longer if it is still a little pink.

Remove the chicken from the oven and leave to cool (reserve the juices in the pan). Arrange the salad leaves, coriander and peanuts on four plates. Finely slice the chicken, scatter it over the salad and drizzle with the pan juices.

SERVES 4

seared lamb with almond salad

50 g (1¾ oz/heaped ½ cup) flaked almonds, toasted and finely chopped
1 garlic clove, crushed
1 handful flat-leaf (Italian) parsley, roughly chopped
10 basil leaves, roughly chopped
3 ripe roma (plum) tomatoes, finely chopped
¼ red onion, finely diced
3 tablespoons extra virgin olive oil
2 x 300 g (10½ oz) lamb backstraps or loin fillets, trimmed
1 tablespoon olive oil

To make the almond salad, put the almonds, garlic, parsley, basil, tomato, onion and extra virgin olive oil in a bowl and season liberally with sea salt and freshly ground black pepper. Toss to combine and set aside.

Put the lamb fillets in a bowl with the olive oil and toss a few times to thoroughly coat the lamb. Heat a non-stick frying pan over high heat and cook the lamb fillets for 3 minutes on each side. Transfer to a plate, season with sea salt, cover loosely with foil and allow to rest for a few minutes.

Spoon the almond salad into the centre of four plates. Slice the lamb fillets on the diagonal, arrange the slices over the salad and pour any meat juices from the resting over the top.

SERVES 4

lamb salad with walnut pesto

1 handful basil
1 handful flat-leaf (Italian) parsley
50 g (1¾ oz/½ cup) grated parmesan cheese
1 garlic clove
100 g (3½ oz/1 cup) walnuts
170 ml (5½ fl oz/⅔ cup) olive oil
250 g (9 oz) cherry tomatoes or truss tomatoes
2 x 300 g (10½ oz) lamb backstraps or loin
    fillets, trimmed
2 baby cos (romaine) lettuces, cut into quarters

Preheat the oven to 180°C (350°F/Gas 4). Put the basil, parsley, parmesan, garlic and walnuts in a food processor with the olive oil and blend to a chunky pesto. Transfer to a bowl and season to taste with sea salt and freshly ground black pepper.

Put the whole tomatoes on a baking tray and roast for 10 minutes, or until they start to split.

Heat a heavy-based frying pan over high heat and sear the lamb fillets for 2 minutes on each side. Put them on a baking tray and bake for 5 minutes, then transfer to a plate, season with sea salt, cover loosely with foil and leave to rest for 5 minutes.

Divide the lettuce quarters among four warmed plates. Slice the lamb on the diagonal and arrange over the lettuce, then top with the roasted tomatoes and a large spoonful of the pesto. Serve drizzled with a little of the pesto oil.

SERVES 4

sesame duck salad

1 whole Chinese roasted duck
600 g (1 lb 5 oz) Chinese cabbage, finely sliced
2 handfuls parsley, roughly chopped
20 mint leaves, finely chopped
1 red capsicum (pepper), finely diced
8 spring onions (scallions), finely sliced
2 tablespoons Chinese black vinegar
2 tablespoons olive oil
1 teaspoon sesame oil
1 teaspoon soy sauce
4 tablespoons sesame seeds

Remove the skin from the duck and, using a pair of kitchen scissors, cut it into thin strips. Put the strips on a baking tray and cook under a hot grill (broiler) for 2–3 minutes, or until crisp. Remove and drain on paper towels.

Pull the flesh from the duck and finely shred it. Toss it in a large bowl with the crispy duck skin, cabbage, parsley, mint, capsicum and spring onion.

In a small bowl, mix together the vinegar, olive oil, sesame oil and soy sauce, then pour over the salad. Toss well, then pile onto a serving platter or into individual bowls.

Put the sesame seeds in a small frying pan over medium heat. As soon as they start to turn golden, take them off the heat and spoon them over the salad.

SERVES 4–6

sesame greens

350 g (12 oz/2 bunches)
   asparagus spears
200 g (7 oz) snow peas (mangetout)
2 baby bok choy (pak choy)
1 teaspoon cornflour (cornstarch)
125 ml (4 fl oz/½ cup) water
3½ tablespoons oyster sauce
1½ tablespoons mirin
1 teaspoon sugar
1 tablespoon sesame seeds
1 tablespoon lime juice

Trim the asparagus spears, then slice each
one in half along its length. Trim the snow
peas, and cut the bok choy into quarters.

Dissolve the cornflour in the water and
pour the mixture into a wok or heavy-
based saucepan. Stir in the oyster sauce,
mirin and sugar.

Put the wok over high heat and, when the
sauce begins to bubble, add the green
vegetables and the sesame seeds and toss
for 2–3 minutes, or until the vegetables are
just tender and cooked through.

Drizzle with lime juice, toss again, then pile
onto a serving platter.

SERVES 4

crab and green bean salad

50 g (1¾ oz/⅓ cup) peanuts
2 tablespoons grated palm sugar or
    soft brown sugar
2 tablespoons fish sauce
4 tablespoons lime juice
2 spring onions (scallions), thinly sliced
2 large red chillies, seeded and
    finely sliced
1 tablespoon finely chopped lemon grass,
    white part only
200 g (7 oz) green beans, trimmed,
    blanched and sliced on the diagonal
150 g (5½ oz/1⅔ cups) bean sprouts
150 g (5½ oz/1½ cups) fresh crabmeat
1 handful coriander (cilantro),
    roughly chopped
10 mint leaves, roughly chopped

Put the peanuts in a small saucepan over medium heat and dry-fry for 2–3 minutes, or until they turn golden brown. Take them off the heat to cool a little, then put them in a blender or food processor and blend until finely chopped.

Put the sugar, fish sauce and lime juice in a large bowl and stir until the sugar has dissolved. Add all the remaining ingredients, including the toasted peanuts, and toss well.

SERVES 4

pumpkin and hazelnut salad

1 kg (2 lb 4 oz) jap (kent) pumpkin
1 tablespoon vegetable oil
100 g (3½ oz/¾ cup) hazelnuts
3 tablespoons tahini
125 g (4½ oz/½ cup) plain yoghurt
1 teaspoon ground cumin
½ teaspoon finely chopped garlic
1 tablespoon lemon juice
200 g (7 oz/2 small bunches) rocket (arugula),
    stalks removed
1 tablespoon olive oil
1 teaspoon red wine vinegar

Preheat the oven to 180°C (350°F/Gas 4). Peel the pumpkin and cut it
into bite-sized chunks. Toss them in a bowl with the vegetable oil and
season with sea salt and freshly ground black pepper. Spread the
pumpkin on a baking tray and roast for 20 minutes, or until golden
brown. Meanwhile, roast the hazelnuts on another baking tray for
5 minutes, or until the skins start splitting. Remove and allow to cool.

Mix the tahini, yoghurt, cumin, garlic and lemon juice to a smooth
paste, then season to taste.

Rub the skins off the cooled hazelnuts and roughly chop the nuts.
Put them in a bowl with the rocket and add the olive oil and vinegar.
Toss together, then divide the leaves among four plates. Top with
the pumpkin chunks and dollop with the tahini mixture.

SERVES 4

capsicum relish on baby cos

3 whole red capsicums (peppers)
2 tablespoons finely diced red onion
2 tablespoons currants
15 mint leaves, finely sliced
15 basil leaves, finely sliced
2 tablespoons extra virgin olive oil
1 teaspoon balsamic vinegar
20 small cos (romaine) lettuce leaves
70 g (2½ oz) goat's cheese

To make the capsicum relish, roast the capsicums in a hot oven or over a gas flame until the skins are charred and black. Put them in a bowl, cover with plastic wrap and leave to cool. Peel away the seeds, membranes and blackened skin, then finely dice the flesh and place in a bowl. Add the red onion, currants, mint leaves, basil leaves, olive oil and balsamic vinegar. Gently mix together and season to taste.

Wash and dry the lettuce. Spoon a heaped teaspoon of the capsicum relish into each leaf, then crumble goat's cheese over the top.

MAKES 20

lentil and beetroot salad

4 beetroot (beets) (about 150 g/5½ oz each), washed
   but not peeled
100 g (3½ oz/½ cup) puy lentils or tiny blue-green lentils
½ teaspoon sea salt
1 teaspoon balsamic vinegar
1 tablespoon extra virgin olive oil
juice of 1 orange
100 g (3½ oz/2⅓ cups) baby rocket (arugula) leaves
100 g (3½ oz) marinated goat's cheese

Preheat the oven to 200°C (400°F/Gas 6). Sit the beetroot in a roasting
tin and pour in 250 ml (9 fl oz/1 cup) of water. Cover with foil and
bake for 1 hour, or until a knife passes easily through the beetroot.
Remove the beetroot from the tin and leave to cool.

Meanwhile, put the lentils in a saucepan with 500 ml (17 fl oz/2 cups)
of water. Add the sea salt and bring to the boil, then reduce the heat
and simmer for 20–30 minutes, or until the lentils are tender. Drain off
any excess water, tip the lentils into a bowl and stir in the vinegar
and olive oil.

Wearing rubber gloves to stop your hands staining, peel the skins from
the beetroot — they should slip free quite easily. Cut the bulbs into
wedges, put them in a bowl and pour the orange juice over the top.

Scatter the rocket leaves on a serving platter and arrange the beetroot
wedges on top. Spoon the lentils over the top, season with a little sea
salt and freshly ground black pepper and drizzle with any remaining
orange and beetroot juice. Crumble the goat's cheese over the top.

SERVES 4

chicken and pine nut salad

1 tablespoon sea salt
2 boneless, skinless chicken breasts
1 egg yolk
zest and juice of 1 lemon
125 ml (4 fl oz/½ cup) light olive oil
2 anchovy fillets, finely chopped
3 tablespoons small salted capers, rinsed and drained
3 tablespoons pine nuts, toasted
3 tablespoons currants
1 very large handful flat-leaf (Italian) parsley, roughly chopped
warm crusty bread, to serve

Put a large pot of water over high heat, add the sea salt and bring to the boil. Add the chicken breasts, then cover the pot and take it off the heat for 40 minutes — during this time the residual heat will gently poach the chicken. Lift the chicken out of the water and allow to cool before shredding the meat.

In a small bowl, whisk together the egg yolk and lemon juice. Slowly add the olive oil, whisking continually to form a thick, creamy mayonnaise. Fold the anchovies through and season with salt and freshly ground black pepper.

Toss the shredded chicken in a large bowl with the lemon zest, capers, pine nuts, currants and parsley. Mix the anchovy mayonnaise through the salad, then spoon into four bowls and serve with warm crusty bread.

SERVES 4

tuna salad in lettuce cups

2 eggs, at room temperature
1 teaspoon red wine vinegar
1 teaspoon dijon mustard
3 tablespoons olive oil
3 tablespoons finely grated
parmesan
100 g (3½ oz) drained tinned tuna
1 celery stalk, diced
10 pitted kalamata olives,
roughly chopped
2 handfuls flat-leaf (Italian) parsley,
roughly chopped
10 cherry tomatoes
20 small mignonette lettuce leaves

Bring a saucepan of water to the boil and add the eggs. Simmer for 5 minutes, then remove the eggs and leave to cool.

In a bowl, whisk the red wine vinegar with the mustard, then slowly whisk in the olive oil. Peel and finely chop the eggs, then add them to the dressing with the grated parmesan, tuna, celery, olives and parsley. Season to taste and stir to combine.

Cut the cherry tomatoes into quarters. Spoon a heaped teaspoon of the salad into each lettuce leaf and garnish with the cherry tomato quarters.

MAKES 20

ma hor on betel leaves

2 garlic cloves, roughly chopped
1 handful coriander (cilantro) leaves
½ teaspoon drained green
    peppercorns in brine
1 teaspoon finely grated fresh ginger
2 spring onions (scallions),
    finely chopped
2 tablespoons peanut oil
150 g (5½ oz) minced (ground) pork
75 g (2½ oz/1 cup) prawn
    (shrimp) meat
2 makrut (kaffir lime) leaves,
    finely sliced
1½ tablespoons grated palm sugar
    or soft brown sugar
1½ tablespoons fish sauce
20 fresh betel leaves

Put the garlic in a blender or food
processor with coriander, peppercorns,
ginger, spring onions and peanut oil. Blend
to a smooth paste.

Heat a frying pan over medium heat, add
the herb paste and cook for 2 minutes. Add
the pork and prawn meat and cook, stirring,
for 5 minutes, or until meat has coloured.
Add the makrut, sugar and fish sauce.

Reduce the heat and cook for 2–3 minutes,
or until slightly sticky. Allow to cool, then
spoon onto the betel leaves, 1 tablespoon
at a time.

MAKES 20

san choy bau

2 iceberg lettuces
2 tablespoons peanut oil
2 teaspoons sesame oil
500 g (1 lb 2 oz) minced (ground) pork
2 tablespoons grated fresh ginger
8 spring onions (scallions),
    finely sliced
2 tablespoons soy sauce
2 tablespoons hoisin sauce
200 g (7 oz/1¼ cups) water
    chestnuts, chopped
1 handful coriander (cilantro) leaves

Remove the core and all the dark outer
leaves from the lettuces. Carefully uncurl
the inner leaves, keeping them in neat
cups, then rinse in a large bowl of cold
water and drain.

Heat the peanut oil and sesame oil in
a large non-stick frying pan over medium–
high heat. Add the pork and cook, stirring,
for 8 minutes, or until lightly golden. Stir
in the ginger, spring onions, soy sauce,
hoisin and the water chestnuts. Cook for
2 minutes, then stir in the coriander.

Serve in a warmed bowl, with the lettuce
leaf cups on a side plate.

SERVES 4

salmon wrapped in vine leaves

4 x 150 g (5½ oz) salmon fillets, bones and skin removed
16 preserved vine leaves
250 g (9 oz) cherry tomatoes
185 g (6½ oz/1 cup) instant couscous
1 tablespoon butter
1 handful flat-leaf (Italian) parsley, roughly chopped
2 spring onions (scallions), finely sliced
olive oil, for drizzling
lemon wedges, to serve

Preheat the oven to 200°C (400°F/Gas 6). Rinse the salmon under running water and pat dry with paper towels. Rinse the vine leaves several times to remove some of the saltiness, but leave them slightly wet to make them easier to work with.

Lay four vine leaves on a clean surface with their edges generously overlapping. Lay a salmon fillet in the middle, then wrap the leaves around the fish. Repeat with the remaining vine leaves and salmon fillets to make four parcels. Put them on a baking tray with the whole cherry tomatoes and bake for 15 minutes.

Meanwhile, put the couscous and butter in a large bowl and pour 250 ml (9 fl oz/1 cup) of boiling water over the top. Cover and allow to sit for 5 minutes, then fluff up the grains with a fork. Cover again and leave for a further 5 minutes. When the couscous has absorbed all the water, rub the grains with your fingertips to remove any lumps.

Remove the salmon from the oven. Add the roasted cherry tomatoes to the couscous along with the parsley and spring onion. Lightly toss together. Divide the salmon parcels among four plates and peel the vine leaves open. Spoon the couscous over the middle of the salmon and serve with a drizzle of olive oil and lemon wedges.

SERVES 4

roast pumpkin and tofu salad

700 g (1 lb 9 oz) jap (kent) pumpkin, peeled
2 tablespoons olive oil
grated zest and juice of 1 lime
1 tablespoon fish sauce
1 tablespoon soy sauce
100 ml (3½ fl oz) mirin
2 bunches broccolini (about 400 g/14 oz in total), trimmed
200 g (7 oz) firm tofu, cut into 2 cm (¾ inch) cubes
1 tablespoon sesame seeds, toasted

Preheat the oven to 180°C (350°F/Gas 4). Cut the pumpkin into bite-sized pieces and put them in a large bowl. Add the olive oil and season with sea salt and freshly ground black pepper. Toss until the pumpkin is well coated, then transfer to a baking tray and roast for 20 minutes, or until golden brown and tender.

Put the lime zest, lime juice, fish sauce, soy sauce and mirin in a large non-metallic bowl and stir to make a dressing.

Bring a saucepan of water to the boil. Add the broccolini and blanch for 2 minutes, or until just tender. Drain the broccolini, then add to the dressing along with the pumpkin, tofu and sesame seeds. Gently toss to mix the dressing through.

SERVES 4–6

fried shallot and cashew salad

125 ml (4 fl oz/½ cup) peanut oil
12 French or red Asian shallots, peeled and cut in half
2 large red chillies, seeded and finely chopped
2 garlic cloves
½ teaspoon sea salt
1 tablespoon grated palm sugar or soft brown sugar
2 tablespoons fish sauce
2 Lebanese (short) cucumbers, peeled and diced
250 g (9 oz) cherry tomatoes, cut into quarters
125 g (4½ oz/heaped ¾ cup) cashew nuts, toasted and
    roughly chopped
2 handfuls Thai basil
2 handfuls coriander (cilantro) leaves

Heat the peanut oil in a frying pan over high heat. When the oil begins to shimmer, add the shallots and fry, stirring, for 1½ minutes, or until golden brown. Remove and drain on paper towels.

In a mortar and pestle or small food processor, pound the chilli, garlic and sea salt into a paste. Add the sugar and work it into the paste for about 1 minute, then stir in the fish sauce to make a dressing.

Put the shallots in a large bowl with the cucumber, tomatoes, cashews, basil and coriander. Pour the dressing over and toss to combine. Serve as a side dish with grilled chicken or seared beef.

SERVES 4

rocket and pear salad

200 g (7 oz/2 small bunches) rocket (arugula)
2 beurre bosc pears, thinly sliced
100 g (3½ oz/1½ cups) parmesan, shaved
1 teaspoon white wine vinegar
1 teaspoon dijon mustard
½ teaspoon honey
2 tablespoons olive oil

Trim the stalks from rocket and put the leaves in a salad bowl with the pear and the parmesan. In a small bowl, mix together the white wine vinegar, dijon mustard and the honey.

Slowly whisk in the olive oil, then season with sea salt and freshly ground black pepper and drizzle over the salad.

SERVES 4

119
leaf

lamb skewers with herbed yoghurt

300 g (10½ oz/about 2¼ cups) plain yoghurt
2 spring onions (scallions), finely sliced
1 teaspoon garam masala
1 teaspoon grated fresh ginger
1 garlic clove, crushed
½ teaspoon ground turmeric
½ teaspoon chilli powder
300 g (10½ oz) diced lamb, cut into 3 cm (1¼ inch) cubes
15 mint leaves, finely chopped
25 g (1 oz/1 bunch) chives, finely snipped
baby leaf salad (optional), to serve

Spoon 4 tablespoons of the yoghurt into a bowl and add the spring onion, garam masala, ginger, garlic, turmeric and chilli powder. Stir to combine, then add the lamb, mixing well to ensure all the cubes are well coated. Cover and refrigerate overnight.

One hour before cooking, soak 8 wooden skewers in cold water to prevent scorching.

Mix the remaining yoghurt with the mint and chives, then spoon into four little serving dishes. Thread the lamb onto the soaked skewers and cook on a hot barbecue chargrill plate or chargrill pan for 4 minutes on each side, or until cooked to your liking. Remove from the heat and season with sea salt. Serve with little dishes of the herbed yoghurt and perhaps a baby leaf salad.

SERVES 4

fried tofu salad

300 g (10½ oz) firm tofu
60 g (2¼ oz/½ cup) plain (all-purpose) flour
1 teaspoon sea salt
1 tablespoon sesame seeds
125 ml (4 fl oz/½ cup) peanut oil
2 Lebanese (short) cucumbers, peeled and diced
4 spring onions (scallions), finely sliced on the diagonal
2 ripe roma (plum) tomatoes, diced
1 handful coriander (cilantro) leaves
20 mint leaves, finely chopped
1 tablespoon lime juice
2 tablespoons kecap manis

Sit the tofu on paper towels for 30 minutes to soak up any excess liquid.

Put the flour in a hot frying pan over high heat and toast it, stirring, for 2½ minutes, or until it turns golden brown. Tip the toasted flour into a large bowl and allow to cool, then stir in the sea salt and sesame seeds. Cut the tofu into 12 slices about 5 mm (¼ inch) thick and toss them in the toasted flour mixture.

Heat the peanut oil in a frying pan and fry the tofu over medium–high heat for 2 minutes on each side, or until golden brown — you may need to do this in two batches. Leave to drain on paper towels, then cut each tofu slice into three triangles, or leave in larger slices.

Gently toss the tofu in a bowl with the cucumber, spring onion, tomato, coriander and mint. Season to taste with sea salt.

In a small bowl, mix together the lime juice and kecap manis. Drizzle over the salad and toss once again before serving.

SERVES 4

tofu, broccolini and almonds

300 g (10½ oz) silken tofu
235 g (8½ oz/1 bunch) broccolini
2 tablespoons olive oil
2 teaspoons finely grated fresh ginger
2 garlic cloves, crushed
2 tablespoons soy sauce
2 tablespoons mirin
3 large red chillies, seeded and finely
  sliced into strips
1 tablespoon butter
50 g (1¾ oz/heaped ½ cup) flaked
  almonds

Cut the tofu into 2 cm (¾ inch) cubes and put them in a large bowl. Cut the broccolini in half, then cut the thicker pieces in half along the stalk.

Heat the olive oil in a wok over high heat. Add the ginger and garlic. As soon as they start to sizzle, add the soy sauce and mirin. When the sauce begins to bubble, add the broccolini and stir-fry for 2 minutes.

Add the chilli and stir-fry for 1 minute, then scoop the vegetables over the tofu, leaving the sauce in the wok. Add the butter to the wok, then the almonds. Stir for 30 seconds, or until the sauce thickly coats the almonds, then spoon the almonds over the vegetables.

SERVES 4

sea

summer sands clear blue waters
swimmers and fins salt and spice

CHARGRILLED PRAWNS WITH LIME AÏOLI ▪ MUSSEL AND SQUID SALAD
TANGY SHELLFISH BROTH ▪ PAN-FRIED BREAM WITH PARSLEY SALAD
SEARED SWORDFISH WITH BLACK-EYED PEAS ▪ PICKLED SWORDFISH SALAD
HERBED CEVICHE WITH AVOCADO SALAD
SALMON CARPACCIO ▪ PRAWN AND CHICKEN SALAD
BANANA LEAF FISH ▪ OCEAN TROUT WITH CUCUMBER SALAD
SQUID AND FENNEL SALAD ▪ RED SNAPPER WITH TOMATO SALSA
WHITE FISH CARPACCIO WITH ASIAN SALSA
SQUID WITH RED CAPSICUM SAUCE ▪ MUSSELS IN TAMARIND BROTH
SWEET PICKLED OCEAN TROUT ▪ SWEET AND SOUR PRAWNS
GREEN SAUCE ▪ BLACK BEAN SCALLOPS
STEAMED FISH WITH WATERCRESS SALAD
LIME AND AVOCADO SALSA ▪ SPICED SALMON
SPICY PRAWN SALAD ▪ LIME PICKLE SAUCE ▪ MAURITIAN FISH STEW

chargrilled prawns with lime aïoli

1 large green chilli, seeded
1 garlic clove
1 teaspoon dried oregano
½ teaspoon ground cumin
grated zest and juice of 1 lime
juice of 1 orange
4 tablespoons olive oil
24 large raw prawns (shrimp), peeled
   and deveined, tails intact

lime aïoli
4 garlic cloves
½ teaspoon salt
1 egg yolk
½ teaspoon finely grated lime zest
2 teaspoons lime juice
170 ml (5½ fl oz/⅔ cup) olive oil

Using a mortar and pestle or small blender, grind the chilli, garlic, oregano, cumin, lime zest, lime juice, orange juice and olive oil together to make a marinade. Season with a little sea salt and ground white pepper. Toss the prawns in the marinade, then cover and refrigerate for 1 hour.

Meanwhile, soak 24 small bamboo skewers in cold water for 30 minutes to prevent scorching.

To make the lime aïoli, pound the garlic and salt to a smooth paste using a mortar and pestle. Scrape the paste into a large bowl, then whisk in the egg yolk, lime zest and lime juice. Whisking continually, slowly add the olive oil a little at a time, until you have a thick mayonnaise. Season to taste, then cover and refrigerate until ready to use. Makes about 160 g (5¾ oz/⅔ cup).

Heat a barbecue flat plate, chargrill or grill (broiler) to high. Drain the skewers and thread a prawn onto each one. Cook the prawns for 1½ minutes, or until they just turn pink and start to curl, then turn and cook for a further 1½ minutes, or until just opaque. Serve at once with the lime aïoli.

SERVES 4

mussel and squid salad

1 kg (2 lb 4 oz) black mussels
20 small squid (about 2 kg/4 lb 8 oz in total), cleaned, tentacles removed
3 tablespoons olive oil
250 ml (9 fl oz/1 cup) dry white wine
4 tablespoons white wine vinegar
3 thyme sprigs
zest and juice of 2 lemons
4 ripe roma (plum) tomatoes, roughly chopped
2 garlic cloves, crushed
4 spring onions (scallions), finely sliced
3 tablespoons roughly chopped parsley
olive oil, extra, for drizzling
baby salad leaves, to serve

Clean the mussels under cold running water, scrubbing them to remove any barnacles or bits of hairy 'beard'. Throw away any broken ones, or any open ones that don't close when you tap them. Slice the squid into 2 cm (¾ inch) strips.

Put the olive oil, wine, vinegar and thyme sprigs in a saucepan. Bring to the boil, then reduce to a simmer over low heat. Add the mussels, then cover the pan and cook for 1½–2 minutes, shaking the pan now and then. Using a slotted spoon, remove the mussels as they open and throw away any that remain closed.

Add the squid to the simmering liquid and cook for 2–3 minutes, or until soft and cooked through. Drain the squid, discarding the liquid, and place in a large bowl. Pull the mussels out of their shells and add them to the squid, along with the lemon zest, lemon juice, tomato, garlic, spring onion and parsley. Toss together, then cover and refrigerate for 1 hour. Season with sea salt and freshly ground black pepper and serve with a drizzle of olive oil on a bed of baby salad leaves.

SERVES 4

tangy shellfish broth

8 raw king prawns (shrimp)
3 lemon grass stems
100 g (3½ oz) oyster mushrooms, cut in half
100 g (3½ oz) enoki mushrooms
6 makrut (kaffir lime) leaves
3 roma (plum) tomatoes, finely chopped
2 spring onions (scallions), finely sliced
juice of 3 limes
1 large red chilli, seeded and finely chopped
2–4 tablespoons fish sauce, or to taste
50 g (1¾ oz/½ cup) fresh crabmeat
1 handful coriander (cilantro), roughly chopped
1 handful mint

Peel and devein the prawns, reserving the shells.

Slice off and reserve the white ends of the lemon grass stems, then cut the long green stalks into 2 cm (¾ inch) lengths and flatten them with a cleaver or the end of a heavy-handled knife.

Heat 1 litre (35 fl oz/4 cups) of water in a saucepan. Add the prawn shells and the white ends of the lemon grass and bring to the boil. Once the water has come to the boil, take the pan off the heat and strain the prawn stock into a large bowl to remove the solids.

Pour the prawn stock back into the saucepan, then add the crushed green lemon grass stalks, mushrooms, lime leaves and tomato. Return to the boil, then reduce the heat and simmer for 3–4 minutes. Add the prawns and, when they start to turn pink, add the spring onion, lime juice, chilli, fish sauce and crabmeat. Stir well, then season to taste. Ladle into warmed bowls and serve with a sprinkle of coriander and mint.

SERVES 4 AS A STARTER, OR 2 AS A MAIN

pan-fried bream with parsley salad

1 large handful flat-leaf (Italian) parsley, chopped
250 g (9 oz) cherry tomatoes, cut in half
25 g (1 oz/1 bunch) chives, snipped into
    3 cm (1¼ inch) lengths
½ red onion, finely sliced
2 tablespoons small salted capers, rinsed and drained
zest and juice of 1 lemon
2 tablespoons olive oil
100 g (3½ oz/scant 1 cup) fine semolina
1 tablespoon finely chopped dill
4 x 150 g (5½ oz) bream fillets
2½ tablespoons butter
lemon wedges, to serve

Preheat the oven to 180°C (350°F/Gas 4). To make the parsley salad, put the parsley, cherry tomatoes, chives, onion, capers, lemon zest, lemon juice and olive oil in a bowl and toss well. Season with freshly ground black pepper and set aside.

Put the semolina and dill in a bowl and mix together well. Season with sea salt and freshly ground black pepper.

Rinse the bream under cold running water and pat dry with paper towels. Dip each fish fillet in the semolina mixture and gently press to coat well on both sides.

Heat the butter in a large frying pan over medium heat and fry the bream fillets for 2 minutes on each side, or until lightly golden. Now put them on a baking tray lined with foil and bake for 5 minutes, or until cooked through. Serve with the parsley salad and lemon wedges.

SERVES 4

seared swordfish with black-eyed peas

200 g (7 oz/1 cup) black-eyed peas
3 handfuls flat-leaf (Italian) parsley, roughly chopped
¼ red onion, finely diced
15 mint leaves, finely chopped
3 tablespoons extra virgin olive oil
juice of 1 lemon
1 teaspoon white wine vinegar
1 tablespoon olive oil
4 x 180 g (6 oz) swordfish steaks
2 lemons, cut into wedges

Soak the black-eyed peas in plenty of cold water for 6–8 hours, or overnight. Drain and rinse well, then put them in a saucepan with plenty of water. Simmer over low heat, uncovered, for 45–60 minutes, or until tender — the actual cooking time will depend on how fresh they are. Drain, rinse well and leave to cool.

Toss the black-eyed peas in a bowl with the parsley, onion, mint, extra virgin olive oil, lemon juice and vinegar. Season generously with sea salt and freshly ground black pepper.

Heat the olive oil in a large heavy-based frying pan over high heat and fry the swordfish steaks for 2–3 minutes on each side, or until cooked through. Serve with lemon wedges and the black-eyed pea salad.

SERVES 4

pickled swordfish salad

4 tablespoons olive oil
2 red onions, thinly sliced
2 green chillies, seeded and finely sliced
2 garlic cloves, finely chopped
1 teaspoon ground cumin
2 tablespoons finely chopped lemon
    grass, white part only
500 g (1 lb 2 oz) cherry tomatoes,
    cut in half, or into quarters if large
600 g (1 lb 5 oz) swordfish, cut
    into 1.5 cm (⅝ inch) cubes
1 handful coriander (cilantro) leaves
15 mint leaves, roughly torn
250 ml (9 fl oz/1 cup) lemon juice
baby leaf salad, to serve

Heat the oil in a heavy-based frying pan over medium heat and add the onion, chilli, garlic, cumin and lemon grass. Cook, stirring, for 5 minutes, or until the onion is translucent. Add the tomatoes and cook for 1 minute, or until they are just starting to soften. Take the pan off the heat and allow the tomato mixture to cool completely.

Arrange the raw fish in a single layer in a wide, non-metallic dish. Spread the tomato mixture over the top, then sprinkle with the coriander and mint. Pour the lemon juice over the top, then cover and marinate overnight in the refrigerator. Bring to room temperature and serve with a baby leaf salad.

SERVES 4

herbed ceviche with avocado salad

250 g (9 oz) fillet of very fresh bream
2 limes, juiced
½ teaspoon sesame oil
2 teaspoons grated palm sugar (or soft brown sugar)
2 teaspoons soy sauce
4 tablespoons coconut milk
1 tablespoon finely chopped mint
1 tablespoon finely chopped coriander (cilantro)
1 avocado, finely diced
1½ tablespoons olive oil

Take the bream, wrap it in plastic wrap and freeze for 1 hour. In a non-metallic bowl, mix together the lime juice, sesame oil, sugar, soy sauce, coconut milk, mint and coriander. Using a sharp knife, cut the fish into paper-thin slices and add them to the marinade. Cover and refrigerate for 1 hour.

Put the avocado in a small bowl, drizzle with olive oil and lightly stir to coat. To serve, arrange the fish on four small plates and pile a mound of avocado in the middle of each. Drizzle with a little of the marinade and season with freshly ground black pepper.

SERVES 4

salmon carpaccio

300 g (10½ oz) piece of sashimi-
    quality salmon
2 small Lebanese (short) cucumbers,
    very finely sliced
½ teaspoon sea salt
1 teaspoon mint, finely chopped
1 teaspoon dill, finely chopped
1 teaspoon sugar
1 lemon, juiced
2 tablespoons sour cream
1 teaspoon grated fresh horseradish or
    horseradish cream
a sprig of dill, to serve

Take the salmon, remove any small bones,
then wrap it in plastic wrap and freeze for
1 hour. Meanwhile, in a non-metallic bowl,
toss together the cucumber, sea salt, mint,
dill, sugar and the lemon juice. Cover and
refrigerate for 1 hour.

Using a very sharp knife, cut the chilled
fish into thin slices. Divide among four
plates and spoon the cucumber salad over
the top, reserving any liquid left in the
bowl. In a small bowl, combine the sour
cream and the horseradish. Stir in enough
reserved cucumber liquid to make a thin
dressing, then drizzle over the cucumber
and salmon. Serve garnished with dill.

SERVES 4

prawn and chicken salad

350 g (12 oz) small cooked prawns (shrimp)
1 teaspoon ground cumin
2 teaspoons fish sauce
4 tablespoons lime juice
4 tablespoons olive oil
1 tablespoon sesame oil
15 mint leaves, finely sliced
1 teaspoon sugar
2 cooked boneless, skinless chicken breasts, shredded
1 carrot, grated
100 g (3½ oz) snow pea (mangetout) sprouts
1 telegraph (long) cucumber, peeled, seeded and diced
2 spring onions (scallions), finely sliced
1 baby cos (romaine) lettuce, finely sliced
1–2 tablespoons sesame seeds, toasted

Peel the prawns and put them in a large bowl.

In a small bowl, combine the cumin, fish sauce, lime juice, olive oil, sesame oil, mint and sugar. Stir until the sugar has dissolved, then pour the mixture over the prawns and toss until the prawns are well coated.

Add the chicken, carrot, snow pea sprouts, cucumber, spring onion and lettuce. Lightly toss together, then pile onto a serving platter or into individual bowls and sprinkle with the sesame seeds.

SERVES 4–6

banana leaf fish

2 tablespoons vegetable oil
1 onion, diced
60 g (2¼ oz/⅔ cup) desiccated coconut
¼ teaspoon chilli powder
¼ teaspoon ground turmeric
1 tablespoon wholegrain mustard
4 squares of banana leaf or baking paper, each
    measuring 25 x 25 cm (10 x 10 inches)
4 x 150 g (5½ oz) blue-eye cod fillets
lime wedges, to serve
steamed white rice (Basics), to serve

Preheat the oven to 180°C (350°F/Gas 4). Heat the oil in a non-stick
frying pan over medium–low heat. Add the onion and cook for
5 minutes, or until soft and translucent, then add the coconut, chilli
powder and turmeric. Increase the heat to medium and cook, stirring,
for 2–3 minutes, or until the coconut is golden brown. Transfer to a
small food processor or blender and blend to a smooth paste. Scrape
the coconut paste into a small bowl and stir the mustard through.

If using banana leaves, run them quickly over a hot gas flame to
soften the leaves, or quickly blanch them in a pot of boiling water
for 30 seconds.

Place a square of banana leaf or baking paper on a clean surface and
top with a piece of fish. Season the fish with a little sea salt, then
spread 2 heaped tablespoons of the coconut paste over the top.
Wrap up the parcel firmly and sit it on a baking tray. Repeat with the
remaining ingredients to make four parcels. Bake for 25 minutes, or
until the fish is cooked through. Serve with lime wedges and steamed
white rice.

SERVES 4

ocean trout with cucumber salad

1 teaspoon ground cumin
½ teaspoon ground coriander
½ teaspoon dried oregano
½ teaspoon ground turmeric
¼ teaspoon cayenne pepper
1 garlic clove, finely chopped
finely grated zest and juice of 2 limes
4 x 150 g (5½ oz) ocean trout fillets
3 Lebanese (short) cucumbers
10 mint leaves, finely chopped
1 tablespoon extra virgin olive oil
4 lime wedges

In a non-metallic bowl, mix together the cumin, coriander, oregano, turmeric, cayenne pepper, garlic, lime zest and lime juice. Add the trout fillets, and turn them about to coat all over. Cover and marinate in the refrigerator for 1 hour.

Preheat the oven to 180°C (350°F/Gas 4). To make the cucumber salad, finely slice the cucumbers and put them in a bowl with the mint, olive oil and a sprinkle of sea salt. Set aside.

Sit the trout fillets on a baking tray lined with foil, season with a little sea salt and bake for 10 minutes, or until the flesh flakes when tested with a fork — it should still be a little rare in the middle. Serve with the cucumber salad and a wedge of lime.

SERVES 4

squid and fennel salad

8 small squid (about 750 g/1 lb 10 oz in total), cleaned
   (reserve the tentacles)
2 garlic cloves, crushed
½ teaspoon ground white pepper
3 tablespoons olive oil
3 tablespoons lemon juice
2 fennel bulbs
16 kalamata olives, pitted and roughly chopped
1 handful parsley, roughly chopped
1 tablespoon finely chopped mint
3 tablespoons unsalted butter

Rinse the squid under cold running water and pat dry with paper towels. Cut the tubes along one side and open them out into a flat piece. Using a sharp knife, lightly score the inside surface with crisscross lines — don't cut too deeply, just enough to mark the flesh. Slice into 3 cm (1¼ inch) wide strips and put the strips and tentacles in a non-metallic bowl. Add the garlic, white pepper, olive oil and lemon juice, then toss well to coat. Cover and refrigerate for 1 hour.

Very finely slice the fennel and place in a bowl with the olives, parsley and mint. Season lightly with sea salt and freshly ground black pepper.

Drain the squid, reserving the marinating liquid. Heat 1 tablespoon of the butter in a non-stick frying pan over medium heat and add the squid a few pieces at a time. Cook for 2½ minutes on each side, or until the flesh is opaque, then add the squid to the fennel. Cook the remaining squid in two more batches, adding more butter as needed.

When all the squid is cooked, add the marinating liquid and any remaining butter to the pan and simmer over medium heat until the butter has melted. Pour the pan juices over the salad and toss well.

SERVES 4

red snapper with tomato salsa

250 g (9 oz) cherry tomatoes, cut into quarters
1 teaspoon finely grated fresh ginger
2 tablespoons finely diced red onion
6 basil leaves, finely sliced
1½ tablespoons lime juice
1½ tablespoons coconut cream
2 tablespoons vegetable oil
4 x 200 g (7 oz) red snapper fillets, skin on
lime wedges, to serve

Preheat the oven to 200ºC (400ºF/Gas 6). To make the tomato salsa, put the cherry tomatoes, ginger, onion, basil, lime juice and coconut cream in a small bowl. Mix together and set aside.

Put the oil in a large heavy-based frying pan over high heat. Rinse the snapper fillets in cold water and pat dry with paper towels. Season liberally with sea salt and put the fillets, skin side down, in the hot pan. Sear for 1–2 minutes, or until the skin is crisp and golden, then turn the fillets over.

Lift the fish, skin side up, onto a baking tray lined with foil. Bake for 8–10 minutes, or until cooked through. Lift the fillets into a serving dish, then spoon the salsa over the top and serve with lime wedges.

SERVES 4

white fish carpaccio with asian salsa

250 g (9 oz) piece sashimi-quality
    trevally, snapper or pomfret
1 Lebanese (short) cucumber,
    finely diced
1 large red chilli, seeded and
    finely diced
½ yellow capsicum (pepper),
    finely diced
1 spring onion (scallion), finely sliced
1 tablespoon finely chopped
    coriander (cilantro)
1 teaspoon finely chopped lemon grass
    (white part only)
1 teaspoon finely grated fresh ginger
2 tablespoons lime juice
1 tablespoon fish sauce
1 teaspoon sugar

Take the fish and remove any bones. Wrap
it in plastic wrap and freeze for 1 hour.
Meanwhile, make the salsa. In a bowl, toss
together the cucumber, chilli, capsicum,
spring onion, coriander, lemon grass and
ginger. In another bowl combine the lime
juice, fish sauce, sugar and sesame oil. Stir
until the sugar has dissolved, then pour the
dressing over the salsa and gently mix.

Using a very sharp knife, cut the chilled
fish into paper-thin slices. Divide among
four small plates and spoon the salsa
over the top.

SERVES 4

squid with red capsicum sauce

10 small squid (about 1 kg/2 lb 4 oz in total), cleaned (reserve the tentacles)
¼ teaspoon chilli flakes
140 ml (4½ fl oz) olive oil
1 garlic clove, roughly chopped
1 tablespoon finely chopped oregano
3 roasted red capsicums (peppers), seeds, membranes and skin removed (Basics)
2 tablespoons lemon juice
100 g (3½ oz/2¾ cups) rocket (arugula) leaves
2 Lebanese (short) cucumbers, roughly chopped
2 tablespoons extra virgin olive oil
lemon wedges, to serve

Rinse the squid under cold running water and pat dry with paper towels. Cut the tubes along one side and open them out into a flat piece. Using a sharp knife, lightly score the inside surface with crisscross lines to make the squid curl up during cooking — don't cut too deeply, just enough to mark the flesh. Slice into 3 cm (1¼ inch) wide strips and put the strips and tentacles in a non-metallic bowl. Add the chilli flakes and 3 tablespoons of the olive oil, then toss well to coat the squid. Cover and chill for 1–2 hours.

To make the red capsicum sauce, put the remaining olive oil in a food processor with the garlic, oregano, capsicum and 1 tablespoon of the lemon juice. Add a good pinch of sea salt and blend into a sauce. Set aside.

Put the remaining lemon juice in a bowl with the rocket, cucumber and extra virgin olive oil. Season with sea salt and freshly ground black pepper and toss well. Spoon the sauce onto four serving plates, smoothing it into a pool. Top with the rocket salad.

Working in batches, cook the squid on a hot barbecue grill plate or chargrill pan for 1–2 minutes on each side, or until it turns opaque and sears brown in a few places. Pile the squid on top of the salad and serve with lemon wedges.

SERVES 4

mussels in tamarind broth

2 kg (4 lb 8 oz) mussels
2 tablespoons vegetable oil
1 teaspoon ground coriander
½ teaspoon ground turmeric
1 clove
1 teaspoon finely grated fresh ginger
1 large red chilli, seeded and finely chopped
2 garlic cloves, finely chopped
4 spring onions (scallions), finely sliced
2 tablespoons tamarind purée
150 ml (5 fl oz) coconut milk
juice of 1 lime
1 handful coriander (cilantro) sprigs
steamed coconut rice (Basics), to serve (optional)

Clean the mussels under cold running water, scrubbing them to remove any barnacles or bits of hairy 'beard'. Throw away any broken ones, or any open ones that don't close when you tap them.

Heat the oil in a large saucepan over medium heat. Add the ground coriander, turmeric and clove, then stir in the ginger and chilli. Add the garlic and spring onion and cook for 1 minute, stirring, then add the tamarind purée and 125 ml (4 fl oz/½ cup) of water and bring to the boil.

Add the mussels, then cover and cook for 2 minutes, or until all the mussels have opened, then take the pan off the heat. Scoop the mussels out with a slotted spoon, leaving the tamarind broth in the pan. Throw away any mussels that haven't opened and divide the rest among four serving bowls.

Put the pan back over medium heat and stir in the coconut milk and lime juice. Simmer for 1 minute, then spoon the broth over the mussels and scatter with the coriander sprigs. Serve as is or, for a more substantial meal, serve with side bowls of steamed coconut rice.

SERVES 4

sweet pickled ocean trout

300 g (10½ oz) piece of fresh ocean trout
1 tablespoon grated fresh ginger
4 limes, juiced
10 mint leaves, finely chopped
1 tablespoon soy sauce
1 tablespoon sesame oil
1 tablespoon Japanese pickled ginger, finely chopped
4 tablespoons pickling liquid (from the pickled ginger)
100 g (3½ oz/2¼ cups) baby English spinach leaves
3–4 tablespoons freshly grated daikon
black sesame seeds, to serve

Take the trout and remove any bones and skin. Wrap it in plastic wrap and freeze for 1 hour. Put the ginger in a non-metallic bowl with the lime juice, mint, soy sauce and sesame oil. Add the pickled ginger and the pickling liquid. Mix well.

Using a very sharp knife, cut the chilled fish into thin slices, put them in a non-metallic dish and add the ginger mixture. Cover and refrigerate for 1 hour. Divide the spinach leaves among four small bowls and scatter with the grated daikon. Top with the pickled salmon, sprinkle with black sesame seeds and drizzle with the pickled ginger juices.

SERVES 4

sweet and sour prawns

½ teaspoon cayenne pepper
1 teaspoon ground turmeric
1 tablespoon tamarind purée
20 raw king prawns (shrimp), peeled and deveined, tails intact
2 tablespoons vegetable oil
2 red onions, finely sliced
1 red capsicum (pepper), cut into 1 cm (½ inch) cubes
1 tablespoon grated palm sugar or soft brown sugar
1 tablespoon balsamic vinegar
100 ml (3½ fl oz) coconut milk
1 handful coriander (cilantro) sprigs
steamed white rice (Basics), to serve

Put the cayenne pepper, turmeric and tamarind purée in a non-metallic bowl and stir to combine. Add the prawns and toss until well coated. Cover and refrigerate until ready to cook.

Put the oil in a large heavy-based frying pan over medium–low heat. Add the onion and cook for 20 minutes, stirring occasionally, until the onion is soft and beginning to caramelize. Add the capsicum, sugar and vinegar and cook for a further 2 minutes.

Add the prawns, laying them on their sides in a single layer over the onion mixture, and cook for 1½–2 minutes on each side, or until they are starting to curl up and turn pink — you may need to cook the prawns in two batches if your pan isn't quite large enough to fit them all at once. Serve the prawns and sauce over steamed white rice, drizzled with the coconut milk and scattered with the coriander sprigs.

SERVES 4

green sauce

1 large handful coriander (cilantro) leaves
10 mint leaves
1 tablespoon small salted capers, rinsed and drained
1 garlic clove, crushed
1 long green chilli, seeded and roughly chopped
1 tablespoon lime juice
1 teaspoon fish sauce
4 tablespoons olive oil

Pile the coriander leaves onto a chopping board with the mint leaves, capers, garlic and green chilli. Using a sharp knife, chop all the ingredients together to form a rough paste.

Put the paste in a bowl and add the lime juice, fish sauce and olive oil. Mix together and spoon over baked or steamed blue-eye cod, snapper or john dory.

MAKES ABOUT 75 G (2½ OZ/½ CUP)

black bean scallops

1 tablespoon finely grated fresh ginger
25 g (1 oz/1 bunch) chives, finely snipped
2 tablespoons Chinese salted black beans
½ teaspoon sesame oil
4 tablespoons dry sherry
2 tablespoons lemon juice
100 g (3½ oz/2¼ cups) baby English spinach leaves
750 g (1 lb 10 oz) scallops, with roe
2½ tablespoons butter
lemon wedges, to serve

Put the ginger, chives, black beans, sesame oil, sherry and lemon juice in a bowl and stir lightly to combine. Divide the spinach leaves among four plates.

Remove the membrane and any vein or tough white muscle from the scallops, leaving the roe attached. Rinse well and pat dry with paper towels.

Melt 2 teaspoons of the butter in a large, heavy-based frying pan over high heat. When the butter begins to froth, add the scallops in several batches and sear for 30 seconds on each side, adding the remaining butter as needed. Remove the scallops with a slotted spoon and gently scatter them over the spinach leaves.

Put the frying pan back over high heat. When the pan juices begin to bubble, add the black bean mixture and quickly swirl around the pan for a minute to warm through. Spoon the sauce over the scallops and serve with lemon wedges.

SERVES 4

steamed fish with watercress salad

4 x 150 g (5½ oz) blue-eye cod fillets
1 telegraph (long) cucumber, peeled, seeded
   and finely julienned
2 large handfuls watercress sprigs
2 tablespoons fish sauce
2 tablespoons lime juice
1½ tablespoons white wine vinegar
1 tablespoon grated fresh ginger
1 teaspoon sugar
1 large red chilli, seeded and finely chopped
steamed white rice (Basics), to serve

Fill a large, wide pot with 6 cm (2½ inches) of water and bring it to the boil.

Rest the base of a bamboo steamer in the boiling water. Line a second bamboo basket with a large square of baking paper, sit the fish fillets on the paper and season with a little sea salt. Cover the basket, then sit it on top of the bamboo steamer and allow the fish to steam for 7–8 minutes, depending on the thickness of the fillets.

Meanwhile, toss the cucumber and watercress in a large bowl. In a small bowl mix together the fish sauce, lime juice, vinegar, ginger, sugar and chilli to make a dressing. Stir until the sugar has dissolved, then pour the dressing over the watercress and lightly toss.

Remove the cooked fish from the steamer and arrange on four warmed plates. Top with the salad, drizzle with any remaining dressing and serve with steamed white rice.

SERVES 4

lime and avocado salsa

1 ripe avocado, diced
1 Lebanese (short) cucumber, finely chopped
½ small red onion, finely diced
2 large red chillies, seeded and finely chopped
1 large handful coriander (cilantro) leaves
2 teaspoons fish sauce
2 tablespoons lime juice
4 tablespoons olive oil
1 lime

Put the avocado in a bowl with the cucumber, red onion, chillies, coriander, fish sauce, lime juice and olive oil.

Using a sharp knife, cut the top and base off the lime. Sit the lime on a chopping board and run the knife down all sides, removing the skin and pith. Run the knife between the membranes to release the lime segments, then finely chop them and gently stir into the salsa, being careful not to mash the avocado. Serve with grilled (broiled) fish.

MAKES ABOUT 600 G (1 LB 5 OZ/2 CUPS)

spiced salmon

4 tablespoons olive oil
1 tablespoon ground cumin
1 teaspoon smoked paprika
1 teaspoon chilli flakes
juice of 2 limes
1 tablespoon small salted capers, rinsed and drained
1 tablespoon finely chopped preserved lemon rind
2 tablespoons finely chopped coriander (cilantro)
4 x 150 g (5½ oz) salmon steaks
steamed couscous (Basics), to serve
small mint leaves, to serve

Put the olive oil, cumin, paprika, chilli flakes, lime juice, capers, preserved lemon rind and coriander in a bowl and stir to combine. Line a baking tray with foil and lay the salmon steaks over the top. Spoon the spice mixture over the salmon, then cover with plastic wrap and refrigerate for 1 hour.

Preheat the oven to 180°C (350°F/Gas 4). Bake the salmon for 10 minutes, or until cooked to your liking. Serve with steamed couscous and a scattering of mint.

SERVES 4

spicy prawn salad

20 cooked prawns (shrimp), peeled and deveined
1 large red chilli, seeded and finely chopped
½ teaspoon cayenne pepper
½ teaspoon ground cumin
1 tablespoon finely grated fresh ginger
2 spring onions (scallions), finely sliced
2 tablespoons lime juice
4 tablespoons olive oil
1 handful coriander (cilantro) leaves
2 small avocados, diced
steamed couscous (Basics), to serve

Put the prawns in a bowl with the chilli, cayenne pepper, cumin, ginger, spring onion, lime juice and olive oil.

Toss to coat the prawns well, then add the coriander and avocado and season to taste. Lightly toss again and serve on a bed of steamed couscous.

SERVES 4

lime pickle sauce

generous handful flat-leaf
  (Italian) parsley
4 anchovies
1 teaspoon small salted capers,
  drained and rinsed
10 mint leaves
2 tablespoons Indian lime pickle
4 tablespoons light olive oil

Put the parsley in a food processor with
the anchovies, capers, mint leaves, lime
pickle and olive oil. Blend into a sauce.

Serve with grilled (broiled) white fish, such
as blue-eye cod, and boiled potatoes.

MAKES ABOUT 75 G (2½ OZ/½ CUP)

mauritian fish stew

2 dried limes
1 tablespoon olive oil
1 tablespoon ground cumin
1 tablespoon ground turmeric
1 garlic clove, crushed
1 large red chilli, seeded and finely chopped
½ vanilla bean
2 large ripe tomatoes, cut into 1 cm (½ inch) cubes
1 green capsicum (pepper), cut into 1 cm (½ inch) cubes
800 g (1 lb 12 oz) sea perch, kingfish or cod,
   cut into 3 cm (1¼ inch) wide strips
1 handful coriander (cilantro) sprigs
lime wedges, to serve

Pierce the dried limes several times with a needle. Heat the olive oil in a large heavy-based frying pan over medium heat and add the cumin, turmeric and garlic. Stir until the spices begin to brown, then add the dried limes, chilli, vanilla bean, tomato, capsicum and 500 ml (17 fl oz/2 cups) of water. Simmer over low heat for 20 minutes to allow the flavours to develop. Season to taste with sea salt.

Add the fish strips, then cover and cook for a further 10 minutes, or until the fish is cooked through. Divide the fish among four bowls and spoon the broth over the top. Scatter with coriander sprigs and serve with lime wedges.

SERVES 4

husk

golden grains slippery noodles bowls of bounty savoury and sweet

BREAKFAST BARS • PINEAPPLE AND LIME MUFFINS

FRIED EGG AND AROMATIC RICE • BERRY BREAKFAST TRIFLE

CINNAMON PIKELETS • SLICED LEG HAM WITH BURGHUL SALAD

BOILED EGG AND QUINOA SALAD

FRESH TOMATO PASTA • CITRUS COUSCOUS

CRUNCHY NOODLE SALAD • CAPSICUM CURRY

NUTTY RICE • SIMMERED VEGETABLES AND TOFU

TUNA AND QUINOA SALAD • FRESH EGG NOODLE SALAD

BUCKWHEAT NOODLE AND HERB SALAD

CARAMELIZED CHICKEN BREAST

SEARED BEEF AND NOODLE SALAD

SHIITAKE BROTH WITH SOMEN NOODLES

RICE NOODLE ROLLS WITH GINGER CHICKEN

CRAB AND LEMON PASTA

CHOCOLATE AND HAZELNUT COOKIES

BERRY SHORTCAKES • GINGER PANNA COTTA

COCONUT AND PASSIONFRUIT BAVAROIS

FRAGRANT PEACH TART • CHOCOLATE PLUM CAKE

breakfast bars

150 g (5½ oz) butter
175 g (6 oz/½ cup) honey
200 g (7 oz/2 cups) rolled
    (porridge) oats
60 g (2¼ oz/1 cup) shredded coconut
1 teaspoon baking powder
3 tablespoons sesame seeds
200 g (7 oz/¾ cup) pitted
    prunes, chopped
100 g (3½ oz/⅔ cup) dried
    peaches, chopped
75 g (2½ oz/½ cup) currants
3 eggs

Preheat the oven to 170°C (325°F/Gas 3).
Line a 23 x 32 cm (9 x 12¾ inch) sandwich
tin with baking paper.

Put the butter and honey in a small
saucepan over medium heat and stir until
the butter has melted.

Toss the oats, coconut, baking powder and
sesame seeds together in a large bowl. Add
the prunes, peaches and currants and mix
well. Add the warm honey mixture and
eggs and stir to combine, then spoon evenly
into the sandwich tin.

Bake for 25–30 minutes, or until the mixture
is cooked through and the top is golden
brown. Remove from the oven and allow to
cool in the tin before cutting into 12 bars.

MAKES 12

pineapple and lime muffins

215 g (7½ oz/1¾ cups) plain
    (all-purpose) flour
2 heaped teaspoons baking powder
165 g (5¾ oz/¾ cup) sugar
¼ teaspoon ground cardamom
pinch of ground cloves
115 g (4 oz/1¼ cups) desiccated
    coconut
2 tablespoons unsalted butter, melted
125 ml (4 fl oz/½ cup) coconut milk
grated zest and juice of 2 limes
2 eggs
190 g (6¾ oz/1 cup) diced
    fresh pineapple

Preheat the oven to 180°C (350°F/Gas 4).
Sift the flour, baking powder and a pinch of
salt into a mixing bowl. Stir in the sugar,
cardamom, cloves and coconut.

Make a well in the centre and add the
melted butter, coconut milk, lime zest, lime
juice and eggs. Mix until just combined,
then fold the pineapple through.

Spoon into 10 holes of a greased standard
muffin tin and bake for 25 minutes, or until
a skewer inserted in the middle comes
out clean.

MAKES 10

fried egg and aromatic rice

2 tablespoons butter
2 garlic cloves, crushed
1 red onion, finely diced
1 tablespoon finely chopped lemon grass,
white part only
1 tablespoon finely chopped fresh ginger
370 g (13 oz/2 cups) cooked basmati rice
2 tablespoons olive oil
4 eggs
2 handfuls coriander (cilantro) leaves,
roughly chopped
1 handful parsley, roughly chopped
25 g (1 oz/1 bunch) chives, finely snipped
sweet chilli sauce (Basics), to serve

Melt the butter in a large heavy-based saucepan or wok over medium
heat. Add the garlic, onion, lemon grass and ginger and cook, stirring
often, for 5 minutes, or until the onion is soft and lightly golden. Add
the rice and cook, stirring, for 5 minutes, or until all the ingredients are
well combined and the rice is starting to stick to the base of the pan.
Remove from the heat and set aside.

Heat the olive oil in a large frying pan over medium–high heat and fry
the eggs to your liking. Stir the coriander, parsley and chives through
the rice and divide among four shallow bowls. Top each bowl with
a fried egg and serve with sweet chilli sauce.

SERVES 4

berry breakfast trifle

200 g (7 oz/2 cups) rolled (porridge) oats
250 ml (9 fl oz/1 cup) apple juice
500 g (1 lb 2 oz/3⅓ cups) strawberries, hulled
3 teaspoons honey
125 g (4½ oz/½ cup) plain yoghurt
150 g (5½ oz/1 cup) blueberries

Put the oats and apple juice in a bowl, mix well, then cover with plastic wrap. Cover and refrigerate for at least 1 hour or overnight, to allow the oats to soak.

Mash half the strawberries with the honey, then mix them through the soaked oats along with the yoghurt. Slice the remaining strawberries.

Spoon half the oat mixture into four serving glasses, and top with half the berries. Cover with the remaining oat mixture, then top with the remaining berries.

SERVES 4

cinnamon pikelets

1½ tablespoons lime juice
100 ml (3½ fl oz) maple syrup
125 g (4½ oz/1 cup) plain
(all-purpose) flour
1 teaspoon ground cinnamon
1 heaped teaspoon baking powder
2 tablespoons caster (superfine) sugar
1 egg, whisked
185 ml (6 fl oz/¾ cup) milk
1 banana, sliced, to serve

Mix the lime juice with the maple syrup and set aside. In a large bowl, mix together the flour, cinnamon, baking powder and sugar and make a well in the centre. Stir in the egg, whisked with the milk, to make a smooth batter — if it is too thick, stir in an extra 2 tablespoons milk.

Put a non-stick frying pan over medium heat and melt just enough butter to coat. Spoon in enough batter to form three 7–8 cm (3 inch) pikelets (griddle cakes). Cook for 20–30 seconds, or until the top begins to bubble, then flip and cook for 30 seconds, then remove. Repeat with the remaining batter, adding more butter to the pan each time.

Serve layered with banana slices and drizzled with the maple and lime syrup.

SERVES 4

sliced leg ham with burghul salad

10 bulb spring onions (scallions)
1 tablespoon balsamic vinegar
1 tablespoon olive oil
1 tablespoon caster (superfine) sugar
500 g (1 lb 2 oz) cherry tomatoes
90 g (3¼ oz/½ cup) burghul (bulgur)
1 teaspoon ground cumin
zest and juice of 1 lemon
2 tablespoons extra virgin olive oil
2 handfuls flat-leaf (Italian) parsley, roughly chopped
8–12 slices leg ham, off the bone

Preheat the oven to 180°C (350°F/Gas 4). Trim the onions and slice them in half lengthways. Toss them in a bowl with the vinegar, olive oil and sugar until all the onions are thoroughly coated. Spread them on a baking tray lined with foil and bake for 25 minutes, or until golden brown.

Add the cherry tomatoes to the baking tray and roast for another 5–10 minutes, or until the skins are starting to split. Remove the tomatoes from the oven.

Put the burghul and cumin in a bowl and cover with 125 ml (4 fl oz/ ½ cup) of boiling water. Leave to sit for 10 minutes, to allow the grains to soak up the water.

Add the roasted onions and tomatoes, lemon zest, lemon juice, extra virgin olive oil and parsley. Season to taste with sea salt and freshly ground black pepper and toss to combine. Divide the ham among four plates and spoon the salad over the top.

SERVES 4

boiled egg and quinoa salad

1 egg yolk
1 tablespoon lemon juice
125 ml (4 fl oz/½ cup) light olive oil
2 anchovy fillets, finely chopped
4 eggs, at room temperature
100 g (3½ oz/½ cup) quinoa
75 g (2½ oz/2¼ cups) wild rocket
    (arugula) leaves
1 tablespoon finely snipped chives

In a small bowl, whisk together the egg yolk and lemon juice, then slowly whisk in the oil to make a dressing. Whisk in the anchovies, then season to taste with sea salt and freshly ground black pepper.

Bring a saucepan of water to the boil and add the eggs. Boil the eggs for 5 minutes, then lift them out of the water and leave to cool.

Put the quinoa in a saucepan and cover with 500 ml (17 fl oz/2 cups) of water. Bring to the boil, then reduce the heat and simmer for 5 minutes, or until the grains are cooked through. Drain the quinoa, tip it into a bowl and stir through half the anchovy dressing.

Arrange a nest of rocket leaves on four plates, then spoon a pile of quinoa into the middle. Peel and halve the eggs and sit them on the quinoa. Drizzle with the remaining dressing and sprinkle with chives.

SERVES 4

fresh tomato pasta

4 medium–large, very ripe tomatoes
1 teaspoon sea salt
2 tablespoons small salted capers,
    rinsed and drained
15 basil leaves, finely chopped
1 handful flat-leaf (Italian) parsley,
    roughly chopped
500 g (1 lb 2 oz) casareccia or penne
75 g (2½ oz/¾ cup) finely grated
    parmesan cheese
3 tablespoons olive oil
20 niçoise olives
finely grated parmesan cheese, extra,
    to serve

Chop the tomatoes and put them in a bowl with the sea salt, capers, basil and parsley. Stir gently to coat the tomatoes, then set aside.

Bring a large pot of salted water to the boil and cook the pasta until al dente. Drain the pasta, then return to the warm pot. Add the parmesan and olive oil and stir a few times, before adding the tomatoes. Season with freshly ground black pepper, toss together, then divide among four pasta bowls. Scatter with the olives and sprinkle with some extra parmesan.

SERVES 4

citrus couscous

185 g (6½ oz/1 cup) instant couscous
1 teaspoon grated orange zest
juice of 1 orange
1 teaspoon grated lemon zest
juice of 1 lemon
2 tablespoons olive oil
2 tablespoons finely chopped preserved lemon rind
2 Lebanese (short) cucumbers, peeled and finely diced
20 basil leaves

Put the couscous in a large bowl and pour 250 ml (9 fl oz/1 cup) of boiling water over the top. Cover and allow to sit for 5 minutes, then fluff up the grains with a fork. Cover again and leave for a further 5 minutes. When the couscous has absorbed all the water, rub the grains with your fingertips to remove any lumps.

In a small bowl, combine the orange zest, orange juice, lemon zest, lemon juice, olive oil and preserved lemon rind. Pour the mixture over the couscous, add the cucumber and basil and toss to combine. Season with sea salt and freshly ground black pepper. Serve with smoked or roast chicken or chargrilled fish.

SERVES 4

crunchy noodle salad

1 tablespoon grated palm sugar or soft brown sugar
2 teaspoons balsamic vinegar
1 tablespoon kecap manis
1 large red chilli, seeded and finely chopped
2 garlic cloves, finely chopped
80 g (2¾ oz/½ cup) peanuts, toasted and ground
125 ml (4 fl oz/½ cup) peanut oil
90 g (3¼ oz) dried Chinese egg vermicelli
2 witlof (chicory/Belgian endive), leaves separated
2 Lebanese (short) cucumbers, cut into long, thin strips
2 carrots, peeled and cut into long, thin strips
12 cherry tomatoes, cut in half
100 g (3½ oz) deep-fried tofu, thinly sliced
4 boiled eggs, peeled and cut in half

Put the sugar in a bowl with 3 tablespoons of boiling water. Stir until the sugar has dissolved, then add the vinegar, kecap manis, chilli, garlic and ground peanuts. Stir well to make a peanut sauce.

Heat the peanut oil in a wok or small saucepan over high heat. When it begins to shimmer, add some of the vermicelli by crumbling the nest into broken strands. Fry for a minute or two, or until the threads begin to look golden brown rather than yellow. Remove with a slotted spoon and drain on paper towels — you'll probably need to fry the vermicelli in several batches.

Divide the witlof leaves among four plates and top with the vermicelli. Add the cucumber, carrot, cherry tomatoes and tofu. Top with the boiled egg halves and drizzle with the peanut sauce.

SERVES 4

capsicum curry

2 tablespoons olive oil
2 garlic cloves, crushed
1 tablespoon grated fresh ginger
1 tablespoon black mustard seeds
½ teaspoon cumin seeds
¼ teaspoon ground cloves
½ teaspoon ground turmeric
2 red onions, finely sliced
2 large red chillies, seeded and finely chopped
2 tablespoons tomato paste (concentrated purée)
250 ml (9 fl oz/1 cup) coconut milk
1 red capsicum (pepper), finely sliced
1 green capsicum (pepper), finely sliced
1 yellow capsicum (pepper), finely sliced
2 handfuls coriander (cilantro) leaves
chapatti, steamed white rice (Basics) or nutty
   rice (page 205) to serve

Heat the olive oil in a large saucepan over medium–high heat. Add the garlic, ginger, mustard seeds, cumin seeds, cloves and turmeric. Cook for 1 minute, or until the mustard seeds begin to pop, then add the onion and chilli. Cook, stirring, for 3 minutes, or until the onion has softened.

Stir in the tomato paste, coconut milk and all the capsicum and reduce the heat to low. Cook for a further 20 minutes, or until the capsicums are soft. Season with sea salt if needed, then take the pan off the heat and stir through the coriander leaves. Serve with rice or chapatti.

SERVES 4

nutty rice

2 tablespoons olive oil
1 teaspoon cumin seeds
1 tablespoon sesame seeds
200 g (7 oz/1 cup) basmati rice
1 handful coriander (cilantro) leaves, roughly chopped

Heat the olive oil in a large saucepan over medium heat. Add the cumin and sesame seeds and fry for 1 minute, or until the sesame seeds turn golden brown.

Add the rice and cook for 1 minute, then pour in 500 ml (17 fl oz/2 cups) of water and bring to the boil, stirring occasionally.

Cover the pan and reduce the heat to low. Simmer for 15 minutes, or until the rice is fluffy and cooked through. Quickly stir in the coriander and serve with a capsicum curry (page 202), or chargrilled prawns (shrimp) or fish.

SERVES 4

simmered vegetables and tofu

1 garlic clove, finely sliced
2 tablespoons soy sauce
2 teaspoons sesame oil
125 ml (4 fl oz/½ cup) shaoxing rice wine
125 ml (4 fl oz/½ cup) mirin
2 star anise
1 tablespoon finely sliced fresh ginger
12 fresh shiitake mushrooms, cut in half if large
1 red capsicum (pepper), cut into 1 cm (½ inch) cubes
1 yellow capsicum (pepper), cut into 1 cm (½ inch) cubes
300 g (10½ oz) silken tofu
2 spring onions (scallions), finely sliced on the diagonal
steamed white rice (Basics), nutty rice (page 205)
or brown rice, to serve

Put the garlic, soy sauce, sesame oil, rice wine, mirin, star anise, ginger, mushrooms and all the capsicum in a large saucepan. Add 125 ml (4 fl oz/½ cup) of water and bring to the boil over high heat. Reduce the heat to low and allow the broth to simmer for 10 minutes.

Cut the tofu into 1.5 cm (⅝ inch) cubes and divide among four wide, warmed bowls. Spoon the vegetables and broth over the top. Garnish with spring onion and serve with rice.

SERVES 4

tuna and quinoa salad

150 g (5½ oz/¾ cup) quinoa
2 tablespoons lemon juice
2 tablespoons olive oil
1 tablespoon finely chopped preserved lemon rind
25 g (1 oz/1 bunch) chives, finely snipped
200 g (7 oz) green beans, blanched and cut into
    3 cm (1¼ inch) lengths, on the diagonal
250 g (9 oz) cherry tomatoes, cut into quarters
200 g (7 oz) tinned tuna in oil, drained
40 g (1½ oz/1¼ cups) mizuna or baby salad leaves

Put the quinoa in a saucepan and cover with 500 ml (17 fl oz/2 cups)
of water. Bring to the boil, then reduce the heat and simmer for
5 minutes, or until the grains are cooked through. Remove from the
heat and drain.

Put the lemon juice, olive oil, preserved lemon rind and chives in a
bowl and add the quinoa. Toss together, then add the green beans,
cherry tomatoes and tuna. Toss once more and season to taste with
sea salt and freshly ground black pepper. Divide the salad leaves
among four plates and spoon the tuna and quinoa salad over the top.

SERVES 4

fresh egg noodle salad

200 g (7 oz) fresh egg noodles
45 g (1½ oz/1 cup) Chinese cabbage, finely sliced
2 spring onions (scallions), finely sliced
100 g (3½ oz/1 heaped cup) bean sprouts
1 carrot, julienned
1 red capsicum (pepper), julienned
2 handfuls coriander (cilantro) leaves
3 tablespoons hoisin sauce
1½ tablespoons lime juice
1 teaspoon sesame oil
1 teaspoon sugar
2 tablespoons sesame seeds, toasted, to serve

Bring a large pot of salted water to the boil and add the egg noodles.
Cook until al dente, then drain, rinse and set aside. In a large bowl,
toss together the Chinese cabbage, spring onions (scallions), bean
sprouts, carrot, red capsicum and coriander.

In a small bowl, combine the hoisin sauce, lime juice, sesame oil and
sugar, then pour over the vegetables. Rinse and drain the noodles,
then toss them through the salad and divide among four bowls. Serve
sprinkled with the toasted sesame seeds.

SERVES 4

buckwheat noodle and herb salad

1½ tablespoons soy sauce
1½ tablespoons sesame oil
2 teaspoons balsamic vinegar
1 tablespoon caster (superfine) sugar
2 tablespoons lime juice
1 tablespoon finely chopped lemon
    grass (white part only)
300 g (10½ oz) buckwheat noodles
half a daikon, peeled and
    finely julienned
2 heaped tablespoons fresh ginger,
    finely julienned
1 handful mint
2 handfuls coriander (cilantro) leaves

Put the soy sauce in a large bowl with the
sesame oil, vinegar, sugar, lime juice and
lemon grass. Stir to make a dressing.

Bring a large pot of water to the boil and
add the buckwheat noodles. Cook until al
dente, then drain, rinse and toss them
through the dressing to coat. Add the
daikon, fresh ginger, mint and coriander.

Gently toss together, then pile the noodles
into four bowls.

SERVES 4

caramelized chicken breast

3 tablespoons vegetable oil
4 boneless chicken breasts, skin on
3 French or red Asian shallots, finely chopped
3 tablespoons caster (superfine) sugar
3 tablespoons fish sauce
1 tablespoon finely grated fresh ginger
¼ teaspoon ground white pepper
2 small Lebanese (short) cucumbers, finely sliced
1 small radicchio, leaves separated
25 g (1 oz/1 bunch) chives, finely snipped
20 mint leaves
1 tablespoon lime juice
steamed coconut rice (Basics) or steamed white
rice (Basics), to serve

Heat the oil in a large heavy-based frying pan over medium–high heat. Add the chicken, skin side down, and cook for 3 minutes, or until golden brown. Turn and cook for 2 minutes. Remove the chicken from the pan.

Add the shallots to the pan and cook for 1 minute over medium heat. Add the sugar and cook for 2 minutes, or until the shallots are golden brown. Stir in the fish sauce, ginger and pepper and cook for 1 minute.

Put the chicken back in, skin side up. Cover the pan, reduce the heat to low and cook for 12–15 minutes, or until the chicken is cooked through. Take the pan off the heat and keep the chicken warm while preparing the salad.

In a bowl, toss together the cucumber, radicchio, chives, mint and lime juice. Season with sea salt.

Serve the salad in four large bowls, piled over some steamed coconut or white rice, with thick slices of chicken arranged over the top. Spoon the caramelized shallots and pan juices over just before serving.

SERVES 4

seared beef and noodle salad

zest and juice of 2 limes
zest and juice of 1 orange
2 tablespoons fish sauce
1 teaspoon sesame oil
1 tablespoon grated palm sugar or soft brown sugar
1 garlic clove, crushed
2 tablespoons finely chopped lemon grass, white part only
1 tablespoon julienned fresh ginger
1 large red chilli, seeded and finely sliced
2 tablespoons olive oil
250 g (9 oz) piece of beef sirloin
200 g (7 oz) somen noodles
1 handful coriander (cilantro) leaves
1 handful Thai basil

In a small bowl, mix together the lime zest, lime juice, orange zest, orange juice, fish sauce, sesame oil, sugar, garlic, lemon grass, ginger and chilli. Stir until the sugar has dissolved, then cover the dressing and set aside until ready to use.

Heat the olive oil in a frying pan over high heat and add the beef. Cook on each side for 2–3 minutes, or until well seared. Transfer the meat to a bowl, cover loosely with foil and leave to rest.

Bring a large pot of salted water to the boil. Add the noodles and cook for 2 minutes, then drain and rinse under running water. Put the noodles in a large bowl and pour half the dressing over. Toss well to coat, then divide the noodles among four bowls.

Finely slice the beef and arrange over the noodles. Scatter with the coriander and basil and spoon the remaining dressing over the top.

SERVES 4

shiitake broth with somen noodles

8 dried shiitake mushrooms
1.5 litres (52 fl oz/6 cups) hot water
2 teaspoons dashi granules
3 tablespoons white miso paste
3 tablespoons soy sauce
12 baby corn cobs, chopped
175 g (6 oz/1 bunch) asparagus, chopped
200 g (7 oz) somen noodles
2 spring onions (scallions), finely sliced, to serve

Soak the shiitake mushrooms in 500 ml (17 fl oz/2 cups) of the hot water for 30 minutes. Drain the liquid into a saucepan, finely slice the mushrooms and add them to the pan with the dashi granules, the remaining hot water, the miso paste and soy sauce. Bring to the boil, then reduce the heat and simmer for 10 minutes.

Add the baby corn cobs and cook for 3 minutes, then add the asparagus and cook for 3 minutes. Meanwhile, cook the somen noodles in a large pot of boiling water for 3 minutes, then drain, rinse and divide among four warmed bowls. Spoon the shiitake broth over the top and scatter with spring onions.

SERVES 4

rice noodle rolls with ginger chicken

500 g (1 lb 2 oz) fresh rice noodle sheets,
    at room temperature
1 tablespoon peanut oil
1 teaspoon finely chopped lemon grass, white part only
1 teaspoon finely grated fresh ginger
1 boneless, skinless chicken breast, finely diced
250 g (9 oz) baby English spinach leaves
2 tablespoons finely snipped garlic chives
2 tablespoons vegetable oil
sweet chilli sauce (Basics), to serve

Open out the rice noodle sheets and cut out eight 20 cm (8 inch)
squares. Put them in a bowl, cover with hot water and leave to soften.

Heat the peanut oil in a wok and add the lemon grass, ginger and
chicken. Stir-fry over medium heat for 5 minutes, or until the chicken
is cooked. Add the baby spinach, toss until the leaves are just wilted,
then take the wok off the heat. Allow the mixture to cool, then stir
through the garlic chives.

Drain the noodle sheets and pat dry with paper towels. Spoon the
chicken mixture along the centre of each noodle sheet and roll them
up by folding the edges over each other.

Heat the vegetable oil in a non-stick frying pan. Working in two
batches, cook the noodle rolls for 1 minute on each side, or until
lightly golden. Serve warm with sweet chilli sauce.

SERVES 4

crab and lemon pasta

350 g (12 oz/2½ cups) fresh crabmeat
2 large red chillies, seeded and finely chopped
grated zest and juice of 1 lemon
4 tablespoons extra virgin olive oil
1 handful flat-leaf (Italian) parsley, roughly chopped
300 g (10½ oz/2 bunches) rocket (arugula), stalks removed,
    leaves finely sliced
400 g (14 oz) spaghettini

Put the crabmeat in a large bowl and roughly flake it with a fork. Add
the chilli, lemon zest, lemon juice and olive oil. Season liberally with
sea salt and freshly ground black pepper and stir to combine. Pile the
parsley and rocket over the top.

Bring a large pot of salted water to the boil and add the spaghettini.
Cook until al dente, then drain and add to the crab mixture. Toss well
until the rocket has wilted, then divide among four warmed pasta bowls.

SERVES 4

chocolate and hazelnut cookies

150 g (5½ oz) good-quality
    dark chocolate
4 tablespoons unsalted butter
200 g (7 oz/1 heaped cup lightly
    packed) dark brown sugar
100 g (3½ oz/heaped ¾ cup) plain
    (all-purpose) flour
1 teaspoon natural vanilla extract
55 g (2 oz/½ cup) ground hazelnuts
1 egg
cream, to serve
fresh figs marinated in brown sugar
    and Grand Marnier, to serve

Melt the dark chocolate and butter in a
small saucepan over low heat. Add the
brown sugar and stir for 1 minute, or until
the sugar dissolves. Sift in the flour, then
stir in the vanilla extract and ground
hazelnuts. Add 1 egg, stir to form a thick
dough, then cover with plastic wrap and
refrigerate for 1 hour.

Preheat the oven to 180°C (350°F/Gas 4).
Shape the dough into small walnut-sized
balls and bake on two baking trays lined
with baking paper for 15–20 minutes, or
until they look dry.

Serve with cream and fresh figs marinated
in brown sugar and Grand Marnier.

MAKES 30

berry shortcakes

185 g (6½ oz/1½ cups) plain
     (all-purpose) flour
½ teaspoon salt
2 teaspoons baking powder
4 tablespoons caster (superfine) sugar
100 g (3½ oz) butter
1 egg
icing (confectioners') sugar, whipped
     cream and mixed berries, to serve

In a large bowl, mix together the flour, salt, baking powder and sugar. Add the butter, rubbing it in with your fingertips, then mix in the egg.

Gather the mixture onto a sheet of plastic wrap, roll up into a fat log about 8 cm (3¼ inches) in diameter and chill for 1 hour.

Preheat the oven to 180°C (350°F/Gas 4). Cut the log into eight discs and put them on a baking tray lined with baking paper. Flatten them slightly, then bake for 10–12 minutes, or until golden brown. Remove from the oven and allow to cool on the tray.

Dust with icing sugar and serve with whipped cream and a bowl of strawberries and raspberries.

SERVES 8

ginger panna cotta

400 ml (14 fl oz) cream (whipping)
grated zest and juice of 1 lemon
1 tablespoon finely grated fresh ginger
50 g (1¾ oz/scant ¼ cup) caster (superfine) sugar
1½ gelatine leaves
1 tablespoon Grand Marnier or orange-flavoured liqueur
cardamom almond bread (Basics) or pistachio biscotti (Basics), to serve

Whip 150 ml (5 fl oz) of the cream in a bowl, cover with plastic wrap and refrigerate until needed.

Put the remaining cream in a saucepan with the lemon zest, lemon juice and ginger and heat gently over low heat for 10 minutes, or until slightly thickened — do not let the cream come to the boil. Strain into a bowl.

Soak the gelatine leaves in a bowl of cold water for 5 minutes, or until dissolved to a jellied consistency. Squeeze the excess water from the gelatine leaves and stir them into the warm cream mixture along with the Grand Marnier. Leave for about 40 minutes to cool, then fold through the whipped cream.

Spoon the panna cotta into four small bowls, then cover and refrigerate for 3 hours or overnight. Serve with cardamom almond bread or pistachio biscotti.

SERVES 4

coconut and passionfruit bavarois

250 ml (9 fl oz/1 cup) cream (whipping)
300 ml (10½ fl oz) milk
45 g (1½ oz/½ cup) desiccated coconut
125 g (4½ oz/heaped ½ cup) caster (superfine) sugar
4 egg yolks
2 gelatine leaves
4 passionfruit
cardamom almond bread (Basics) or pistachio biscotti
    (Basics), to serve

Whip the cream in a bowl, cover with plastic wrap and refrigerate until needed.

Put the milk in a heavy-based saucepan over very low heat and stir in the coconut and sugar. Allow the milk to just simmer for 15 minutes, or until reduced and thick, then strain into a bowl through a fine sieve. Using the back of a large spoon, press as much liquid as possible out of the coconut into the bowl.

Whisk the egg yolks in a separate bowl, then whisk in the warm milk. Pour into a clean saucepan and stir over medium heat for 8–10 minutes, or until the mixture coats the back of the spoon. Pour into a clean bowl.

Soak the gelatine leaves in a bowl of cold water for 5 minutes, or until dissolved to a jellied consistency. Squeeze the excess water from the gelatine leaves and add them to the hot milk mixture. Whisk for a few minutes to ensure the gelatine has completely dissolved. Leave for 45 minutes, or until cool.

Fold the cream through the mixture and spoon into four glasses. Cover with plastic wrap and chill for 3 hours, or overnight. Just before serving, slice the passionfruit in half, scoop out the seeds and spoon over the top. Serve with cardamom almond bread or pistachio biscotti.

SERVES 4

fragrant peach tart

6–7 small ripe peaches
25 cm (10 inch) pre-baked shortcrust tart case,
    with 3 cm (1¼ inch) deep sides (Basics)
2 eggs
115 g (4 oz/½ cup) caster (superfine) sugar
4 tablespoons plain (all-purpose) flour
½ teaspoon rosewater
110 g (3¾ oz) unsalted butter
thick (double/heavy) cream, to serve

Preheat the oven to 180°C (350°F/Gas 4). Slice the peaches in half and remove the stones. Slice the flesh into thick wedges and arrange in the base of the tart case, cut sides up.

Crack the eggs into a mixing bowl, add the sugar and beat with electric beaters until pale and fluffy. Fold in the flour and rosewater.

Heat the butter in a saucepan over high heat. When it begins to froth and turn pale golden brown, pour it into the egg mixture and beat for 1 minute. Pour the filling over the peaches and bake for 35 minutes. Cover the tart with foil and bake for a further 15 minutes, or until the filling has set. Allow the tart to cool and serve with cream.

SERVES 8

chocolate plum cake

165 g (5¾ oz/¾ cup firmly packed) dark brown sugar
280 g (10 oz/2¼ cups) plain (all-purpose) flour
185 g (6½ oz) unsalted butter
2 teaspoons baking powder
3 tablespoons dark cocoa powder
¼ teaspoon salt
230 g (8 oz/1 cup) caster (superfine) sugar
3 eggs, lightly beaten
185 ml (6 fl oz/¾ cup) milk
16 small plums (550 g/1 lb 4 oz in total),
    stones removed, cut in half
ice cream or thick (double/heavy) cream, to serve

Preheat the oven to 180°C (350°F/Gas 4). Put the brown sugar in a bowl with 30 g (1 oz/ ¼ cup) of the flour and mix together. Add 3 tablespoons of the cold butter (leave the rest at room temperature to soften) and rub the butter in with your fingertips until the mixture resembles coarse breadcrumbs.

Sift the remaining flour into a mixing bowl along with the baking powder, cocoa powder and salt. Put the caster sugar and softened butter in a separate bowl and cream together using electric beaters, then add the eggs and mix well. Add half the flour mixture, then half the milk, mixing well after each addition. Mix in the remaining flour mixture, then the remaining milk.

Pour the cake batter into a greased 25 cm (10 inch) spring-form cake tin and arrange the plum halves on top, cut sides down. Sprinkle with the brown sugar mixture and bake for 50–60 minutes, or until a skewer inserted in the middle comes out clean.

Remove the cake from the oven and allow to cool before turning out of the tin. Serve with ice cream or cream.

SERVES 10

basics

mix, match and complement

savoury recipes

couscous

185 g (6½ oz/1 cup) instant couscous
1 tablespoon butter

Put the couscous and butter in a large bowl and pour 250 ml (9 fl oz/1 cup) of boiling water over the top. Cover and allow to sit for 5 minutes, then fluff up the grains with a fork. Cover again and leave for a further 5 minutes. Season with a little sea salt and freshly ground black pepper, then rub the grains with your fingertips to remove any lumps. The couscous can be served warm or chilled.

SERVES 4 AS A SIDE DISH

herbed couscous

185 g (6½ oz/1 cup) instant couscous
1 tablespoon butter
1 handful coriander (cilantro) leaves,
    roughly chopped
1 handful flat-leaf (Italian) parsley,
    roughly chopped
finely chopped basil (optional)
finely chopped mint (optional)
finely snipped chives (optional)

Put the couscous and butter in a large bowl and pour 250 ml (9 fl oz/1 cup) of boiling water over the top. Cover and allow to sit for 5 minutes, then fluff up the grains with a fork. Cover and leave for 5 minutes. Season with a little sea salt and freshly ground black pepper, then rub the grains with your fingertips to remove any lumps.

Allow the couscous to cool a little, then stir through the coriander and parsley. To vary the flavour, you can also add finely chopped basil, mint or chives, to suit the dish you are serving the couscous with.

SERVES 4 AS A SIDE DISH

roasted capsicums

2–3 red capsicums (peppers)
olive oil, for brushing

Preheat the oven to 200°C (400°F/Gas 6). Sit a small rack on or over a baking tray or roasting tin. Lightly rub the capsicums with olive oil and sit them on the rack.

Roast the capsicums for 8–10 minutes, or until the skins begin to blister and blacken — you may need to turn them several times so the skins blister all over. (If you have a gas stove you can also blister the skin by carefully putting the capsicums directly over the flame, turning them as the skin blisters.) Put the roasted capsicums in a container, cover with plastic wrap and leave to cool — covering them will make them sweat and make them easier to peel.

Remove the skin from the capsicums by rubbing it away with your fingertips. Cut away the stems and seeds. The flesh is now ready to eat or use.

shaved coconut

This may not be the traditional way of attacking a coconut but it's the easiest way I know of. I have been known to throw them out of second-storey windows, but this can be dangerous to innocent passers-by!

1 coconut

Preheat the oven to 200°C (400°F/Gas 6) and put the coconut on a shallow baking tray and warm in the oven for 5–10 minutes, or until the shell is starting to crack. Remove from the oven and allow to cool.

Using a blunt knife, prise the shell of the cooled coconut open — it should easily split apart. Remove the flesh by wedging the knife between the flesh and the shell. When the flesh has come away, you can shave it using a vegetable peeler, or grate it with a cheese grater.

SERVES 4 AS A SIDE DISH

steamed coconut rice

400 g (14 oz/2 cups) white
    long-grain rice
750 ml (26 fl oz/3 cups) light
    coconut milk
1 pandan leaf, tied in a knot
½ teaspoon sea salt
1 teaspoon butter

Put the rice in a large bowl and cover with water. Stir several times, then drain away the water. Repeat this process several times to remove some of the starch from the rice.

Put the rice and the remaining ingredients in a saucepan and bring to the boil. Reduce the heat to the lowest setting, cover the saucepan and cook for 30 minutes. Discard the pandan leaf before serving.

SERVES 6 AS A SIDE DISH

steamed white rice

200 g (7 oz/1 cup) white
    long-grain rice
435 ml (15¼ oz/1¾ cups) water

Put the rice in a saucepan with a tight-fitting lid.

Cover with the water and add a pinch of sea salt. Bring to the boil, then stir once to ensure the grains have not stuck to the base of the pan.

Cover the pan and turn the heat down to the lowest setting. Cook the rice for 15 minutes, then take the pan off the heat and allow the rice to sit for a further 10 minutes. Just before serving, fluff up the grains with a fork.

SERVES 2–4 AS A SIDE DISH

sweet chilli sauce

5 garlic cloves, peeled

2 large red chillies, green
stems removed

10 cm (4 inch) piece of lemon grass,
trimmed and finely chopped

6 cm (2½ inch) knob of ginger, peeled
and roughly chopped

5 cm (2 inch) knob of galangal, peeled
and roughly chopped

10 makrut (kaffir lime) leaves, cut into
thin strips

1 handful coriander (cilantro) leaves

100 ml (3½ fl oz) Chinese black vinegar

2 tablespoons fish sauce

2 tablespoons soy sauce

345 g (12 oz/1½ cups) caster
(superfine) sugar

Blend the garlic, chillies, lemon grass,
ginger, galangal, lime leaves and coriander
to a rough paste in a mini food processor.
Mix the vinegar, fish sauce and soy sauce
together in a small bowl.

Place the sugar in a saucepan with
4 tablespoons of water and stir over
medium heat until the sugar has dissolved.
Now turn the heat to high and cook for
4 minutes, or until the sugar is beginning
to colour. Keeping a constant watch,
continue boiling the sugar until it is almost
burning and has a wonderful toffee smell.

Quickly add the spice paste and stir for
1 minute, then stir in the vinegar mixture.

Cook for a further 2 minutes, then take the
pan off the heat. Allow to cool, then pour
into a clean glass jar. Cover and refrigerate
until ready to use. The sauce will keep for
several weeks in the refrigerator.

MAKES 330 ML (11¼ FL OZ/1⅓ CUPS)

sweet recipes

cardamom almond bread

3 egg whites
80 g (2¾ oz/⅓ cup) caster
   (superfine) sugar
85 g (3 oz/⅔ cup) plain
   (all-purpose) flour
zest of 2 oranges
90 g (3¼ oz/½ cup) blanched almonds
¼ teaspoon ground cardamom

Preheat the oven to 180°C (350°F/Gas 4).
Grease an 8 x 22 cm (3¼ x 8½ inch) loaf
(bar) tin and line it with baking paper.
Whip the egg whites until they are stiff,
then slowly whisk in the sugar. When the
sugar has been fully incorporated and the
whites are glossy, fold in the flour, orange
zest, almonds and cardamom. Spoon the
mixture into the prepared tin and bake for
40 minutes.

Cool the almond bread on a wire rack.
When the loaf is cold, cut it into thin slices
with a serrated knife and spread them out
on a baking tray. Bake at 140°C (275°F/
Gas 1) for 15 minutes, or until the slices are
crisp. Allow to cool completely on a wire
rack before storing in an airtight container.

MAKES ABOUT 30 SLICES

pistachio biscotti

125 g (4½ oz/1 cup) plain
   (all-purpose) flour
115 g (4 oz/½ cup) caster
   (superfine) sugar
1 teaspoon baking powder
150 g (5½ oz/1 cup) shelled
   pistachio nuts
2 teaspoons grated orange zest
2 eggs, beaten

Preheat the oven to 180°C (350°F/Gas 4).
Mix the flour, sugar, baking powder,
pistachios and orange zest together in
a large bowl. Make a well in the centre and
fold in the eggs to make a sticky dough.

Turn out onto a clean, floured surface.
Divide the dough into two portions and roll
each one into a log about 4 cm (1½ inches)
long. Put them on a baking tray lined
with baking paper, leaving some space in
between to allow for spreading. Bake for
30 minutes, then remove from the oven and
allow to cool.

Reduce the oven temperature to 140°C
(275°F/Gas 1). Using a very sharp bread
knife, cut each loaf into thin slices about
5 mm (¼ inch) thick. Sit the biscuits on
a baking tray and bake for 20 minutes,
turning once during baking. Remove from
the oven and cool on wire racks.

MAKES 30 TO 40 BISCUITS

shortcrust tart case

200 g (7 oz/1⅔ cups) plain
  (all-purpose) flour
100 g (3½ oz) chilled unsalted butter
2 tablespoons chilled water

Put the flour, butter and a pinch of salt in
a food processor and process for 1 minute.
Add the chilled water and process until the
mixture comes together. Wrap the dough in
plastic wrap and refrigerate for 30 minutes.

Grease a 25 cm (10 inch) tart tin or six
8 cm (3¼ inch) tartlet tins. Roll the pastry
out as thinly as possible between two
layers of plastic wrap, then use it to line
the prepared tin or tins. Chill for a further
30 minutes.

Preheat the oven to 180°C (350°F/Gas 4).
Using a fork, prick the pastry case/s over
the base, line with crumpled baking paper
and fill with rice or baking weights. Bake
for 10–15 minutes, or until the pastry looks
cooked and dry. Remove from the oven and
allow to cool.

MAKES 1 LARGE OR 6 SMALL TARTLET CASES

Note: If you are not using the tart case
immediately, it will keep in the freezer
for several weeks. There is no need to
thaw before using — simply put it in the
preheated oven direct from the freezer.

walnut bread

450 g (1 lb/3⅔ cups) plain
  (all-purpose) flour
1 heaped teaspoon bicarbonate of
  soda (baking soda)
1 heaped teaspoon cream of tartar
1 tablespoon sugar
1 teaspoon sea salt
500 ml (17 fl oz/2 cups) buttermilk
4 tablespoons finely chopped walnuts
2 tablespoons butter, melted

Preheat the oven to 200°C (400°F/Gas 6).
Mix the flour, bicarbonate of soda, cream
of tartar, sugar and sea salt together in
a large bowl. Make a well in the centre and
gradually add the buttermilk, combining
to form a soft dough. Slowly fold the
walnuts through.

Brush a 21 x 10 cm (8¼ x 4 inch) loaf (bar)
tin with the melted butter. Put the dough
into the greased tin and pour over any
remaining butter. Bake for 30 minutes.

Reduce the oven temperature to 150°C
(300°F/Gas 2) and bake for a further
30 minutes, or until a skewer inserted
into the centre comes out clean. Turn the
bread out onto a wire rack to cool.

MAKES 1 LOAF

glossary

betel leaf

This delicate green leaf, also known as char plu, is commonly eaten raw in Thai cuisine, where it is often used as a base or a wrapping for the small appetizers known as miang. The leaves are sold in bunches in Thai or Asian speciality shops.

black-eyed peas

Black-eyed peas (sometimes also called black-eyed beans) are small, cream-coloured kidney beans with a distinctive black spot.

black rice

This form of glutinous rice owes its colour to the layer of bran left intact on the grain which colours the rice as it cooks, resulting in a uniformly purplish-black rice. Predominantly used for sweet dishes in Thailand and the Philippines, it is available from Asian food stores.

black sesame seeds

Mainly used in Asian cooking, black sesame seeds add colour, crunch and a distinct nuttiness to whatever dish they garnish. They can be found in most Asian grocery stores. Purchase the seeds regularly, as they can become rancid with age.

buckwheat noodles

A speciality of northern Japan, buckwheat or soba noodles can be made entirely from buckwheat, but are often combined with a percentage of flour. These thin, highly nutritious noodles provide protein, calcium, iron and rutin.

burghul

Popular in the Middle East, burghul (bulgar) is the key ingredient in tabouleh and pilaff. You can buy these wheat kernels either whole or cracked into fine, medium or coarse grains. They are pre-steamed and pre-baked to minimize cooking time.

buttermilk

This cultured, low-fat dairy product is made from skim milk and milk powder and has a tart taste. It is often used in baking as a raising agent and can be found in the refrigerated section of supermarkets.

capers

Capers are the buds from a Mediterranean shrub, preserved in brine or salt. Salted capers have a firmer texture and are often smaller than those preserved in brine. The salted capers have a better flavour, and the salt they are preserved in is a wonderfully flavoured alternative to sea salt.

casareccia

These short lengths of rolled and twisted Italian pasta are traditionally served with a meat sauce. This style of pasta is now commercially produced and is available in most large supermarkets.

chinese black vinegar

This rice vinegar is sharper than white rice vinegars and is traditionally used in stir-fries, soups and dipping sauces. The Chinese province of Chekiang has the reputation for producing the best black vinegars.

chinese salted black beans

These salted black beans can be found either vacuum-packed or sold in tins in Asian food stores. Their strong flavour can be used to bring a rich saltiness to stir-fries and sauces for beef dishes.

chocolate

Couverture is the best-quality chocolate for cooking. This bittersweet chocolate contains the highest percentage of cocoa butter. It is available from gourmet stores and good delicatessens, but if you are unable to obtain chocolate of this standard, it is preferable to use a good-quality eating chocolate rather than a cheap cooking chocolate. Cooking chocolates, on the whole, do not have a good flavour and tend to result in an oily rather than a buttery texture.

coconut

The coconut is a common cooking ingredient in the Pacific, South-East Asia and India. The flesh is often grated or shredded and then dried. Shredding coconut produces small thin strips of dried coconut which are often used decoratively in desserts. Desiccated coconut is finely grated coconut which has been dried. It can be used in savoury as well as sweet dishes. See also shaved coconut (Basics).

crème fraîche

A naturally soured cream that is lighter than sour cream, crème fraîche is available at gourmet food stores and some large supermarkets. Sour cream can usually be used as a substitute.

daikon

Daikon, or mooli, is a large white radish. Its flavour varies from mild to surprisingly spicy, depending on the season and variety. Daikon contains an enzyme that aids digestion. It can be freshly grated or slow-cooked in broths, and is available from most large supermarkets or Asian grocery stores. Select firm and shiny vegetables with unscarred skins.

dashi granules

A common ingredient in Japanese cooking, dashi is a stock base made from dried kelp and flakes of dried bonito (a type of fish). Instant dashi can be bought from Asian food stores. Follow the manufacturer's instructions and simply add water to make an easy stock.

dried chinese egg vermicelli

These very thin noodles are made from wheat flour, water and egg. They are normally packaged in small neat bundles of dried yellow noodles.

dried limes

Traditionally used in Persian cuisine, dried limes are small, black and withered-looking and feel hard and almost hollow. They add an exquisite flavour to dishes and are sold by Middle Eastern grocers.

enoki mushrooms

These pale, delicate mushrooms have long, thin stalks and tiny caps. They are very fragile and need only a minimal cooking time. They are quite bland in flavour but have an interesting texture and appearance, so are ideal for blending with other mushrooms or for adding to Asian stir-fries for an exotic touch.

fine semolina

Semolina is made of coarse granules of durum wheat. Fine semolina has smaller grains and is available from gourmet food stores.

french or red asian shallots

These small onions have a thin, papery skin and grow in bunches. They are also sometimes referred to as eschallots.

galangal

Although a member of the ginger family, galangal has a distinctly different flavour to ginger. Its fragrance is exquisitely perfumed, with a subtle hint of camphor. The root, although similar to ginger in appearance, is quite fibrous and tough, making it difficult to chop. Galangal is most commonly used in the cuisines of Malaysia and Indonesia and comes into its own in the soups of Thailand. It can be bought fresh, or sliced and preserved in brine in bottles from Asian grocery stores.

gelatine leaves

Leaf gelatine is available in sheets of varying sizes. Be careful to check the manufacturer's instructions regarding which ratio of liquid to gelatine sheet to use. If leaves are unavailable, use gelatine powder instead, making sure it is well dissolved in warm liquid during use. Once again, refer to the manufacturer's instructions.

horseradish

Large and white with a knobbly brown skin, horseradish is a root belonging to the mustard family. It is very pungent and has a spicy, hot flavour. It is usually freshly grated as a condiment for roast beef and smoked fish. When commercially produced, horseradish is often blended with cream to give it a smoother texture. Dollop on roast beef or smoked salmon.

indian lime pickle

Lime pickle is available from Indian grocery stores or large supermarkets. It is usually served as a side dish in Indian cooking.

japanese pickled ginger

Japanese pickled ginger is available from most large supermarkets. The thin slivers of young ginger root are pickled in sweet vinegar and turn a distinctive salmon-pink colour in the process. This soft pink colour is often exaggerated to a hot pink colour in commercially produced ginger, due to the addition of food colouring. The vinegar it is pickled in is terrific in sauces where a sweet, gingery bite is called for.

kecap manis

This is a thick, sweet-flavoured soy sauce used in Indonesian cooking.

makrut leaves

The glossy leaves of this South-East Asian tree (also called a kaffir lime) impart a wonderful citrusy flavour to food. Where possible, always use fresh, rather than dried, leaves.

mesclun

Mesclun is a green salad mix originating in Provence, France. It often features a selection of young, small leaves.

mirin

Mirin is a rice wine used in Japanese cooking. It adds sweetness to many sauces and dressings, and is used for marinating and glazing dishes. It is available rom Asian grocery stores and most supermarkets.

miso paste

An important ingredient in Japanese cooking, miso paste is made from fermented soya beans and flavourings such as wheat, rice or barley. It is used as a flavouring and condiment. See also white miso.

mizuna

These tender young salad leaves have a pleasant, peppery flavour.

natural vanilla extract

When using vanilla essence, always ensure it is made from real vanilla and is not labelled 'imitation' vanilla extract or essence. The flavours are quite different, with the imitation being almost acrid in its aftertaste. See also vanilla bean.

niçoise olives

Niçoise or Ligurian olives are small black olives that are commonly used in salads or scattered over prepared dishes. They are not suitable for stoning and making into pastes.

nori

Nori is an edible seaweed sold in paper-thin sheets. To concentrate the flavour, lightly roast the shiny side of the sheets over a low flame or in a hot oven for several minutes. Nori sheets are sold in large supermarkets and Asian grocery stores.

orange flower water

This perfumed distillation of bitter orange blossoms is used to flavour baked goods and drinks. It is readily available from large supermarkets and delicatessens.

oyster mushrooms

These beautifully shaped, delicately flavoured mushrooms are commonly white or a pale, greyish brown, but can also be pink or yellow. They are often also called abalone mushrooms. Their flavour is quite sharp when raw, making them suitable for creamy pasta or stir-fried dishes.

palm sugar

Palm sugar is obtained from the sap of various palm trees and is sold in hard cakes or cylinders and in plastic jars. If it is very hard it will need to be grated. It can be found in Asian grocery stores and large supermarkets. Soft brown sugar can be used instead.

pandan leaf

This fragrant leaf of a type of pandanus tree is widely used in South-East Asian cooking to flavour rice dishes and sweets. It is sold in Asian grocery stores.

papaya

This large tropical fruit can be red, orange or yellow. It contains an enzyme that stops gelatine setting, so avoid using it in jellies. It is sometimes called a pawpaw, but is really part of the custard apple family.

preserved lemon

These are whole lemons preserved in salt or brine, making their rind soft and pliable. Only the rind is used in cooking — the bitter, salty pulp should be scraped out and thrown away. Preserved lemons are available from delicatessens.

puy lentils

Originally grown in the volcanic soils of the Puy region in France, these lentils are highly prized for their flavour and the fact that they hold their shape during cooking.

quinoa

A grain native to South America, quinoa is high in protein and very nourishing as it contains all eight essential amino acids. A wonderful base for salads and hearty sauces, quinoa is an ideal substitute for brown rice and has a similar nutty flavour. It is available from health food stores.

raw caster sugar

Also known as superfine sugar, this is a finer form of raw sugar. It brings a lovely brown tone to the food it is used to sweeten, and a slightly caramel flavour.

rice noodle sheets

These are simply flat sheets of fresh rice noodles, available from Asian grocery stores. The sheets can be cut into strips to make a rough noodle, or wrapped around cooked ingredients to make tasty little parcels.

rice wine vinegar

Made from fermented rice, this vinegar can be clear, red or black. If no colour is specified in a recipe, use the clear vinegar. The clear rice wine vinegar is sweeter and milder than the European vinegars or the darker and sharper-flavoured Chinese black vinegar.

rosewater

The distilled essence of rose petals, rosewater is used in small quantities to impart a perfumed flavour to pastries, fruit salads and puddings. It is available from delicatessens and large supermarkets.

saffron threads

The world's most expensive spice, saffron threads are the orange-red stigmas from a species of crocus plant, which are hand-picked, then dried — a very laborious process. Fortunately, saffron has a very strong flavour, so a very small amount goes a long way. Beware of inexpensive brands — cheap, 'real' saffron does not exist!

sashimi-grade salmon

Salmon sold for making sushi and sashimi is intended to be eaten raw, and so is usually the freshest fish at the markets. Buy a thick piece cut from the centre rather than the narrower tail end.

sesame oil

Sesame oil is available in two varieties. The darker, more pungent, type is made from roasted sesame seeds and comes from China, while the paler, non-roasted variety is Middle Eastern in origin.

shaoxing rice wine

This Chinese rice wine is used to add flavour to braised dishes and sauces. It takes its name from Shaoxing or Shao Hsing, a northern provincial town in China which has been producing rice wine for centuries. Shaoxing rice wine is similar to a fine sherry and is made from glutinous rice.

shiitake mushrooms

These Asian mushrooms have white gills and a brown cap. Meaty in texture, they keep their shape well when cooked. Dried shiitake are often sold as dried Chinese mushrooms.

sichuan peppercorns

These are made from the dried red berries of the prickly ash tree, which is native to Sichuan in China. The flavour is spicy-hot and leaves a numbing aftertaste, which can linger for some time. Dry-fry and crush the berries for the best flavour. Japanese sancho pepper is a close relative and may be used as a substitute.

smoked paprika

Paprika is commonly sold as a dried, rich red powder made from a member of the chilli family. It is sold in many grades, from delicate through to sweet and finally hot. Smoked paprika from Spain adds a distinct rich, smoky flavour to recipes and is well worth looking for if you enjoy introducing these flavours into your favourite dishes.

somen noodles

These thin, wheat-based Japanese noodles are commonly sold dried and in bundles. They are available from Japanese speciality stores, large supermarkets and health food shops.

squid

You can often buy cleaned squid from fishmongers, but if you wish to clean squid yourself, here's how to do it. First remove the body from the head by gently pulling away the tentacles. Ensure the intestines have come away by running your finger around the interior of the tube, removing the plastic–like quill as you do so. Rinse the squid under running water, pulling away the semi-transparent skin. Next, remove the tentacles from the head by cutting through the flesh between the eyes and the tentacles. Feel around the centre of the tentacles for any tough membrane, and the small beak-like mouth. Remove and rinse under running water. Depending on your recipe, you can then cut the cleaned squid into rings using a sharp knife, or slice down one side of the squid, open it into a flat piece and score the softer inside surface with shallow crisscross incisions, then slice it into strips or pieces for cooking.

sumac

Sumac is a peppery, sour spice made from dried and ground sumac berries. The fruit of a shrub found in the northern hemisphere, it is typically used in Middle Eastern cookery. Sumac is available from most large supermarkets and Middle Eastern speciality stores.

tahini

This is a thick, creamy paste made from ground white sesame seeds. It is used to give a strong nutty flavour to Middle Eastern salads or sauces. Tahini is sold in jars in health food stores and most supermarkets.

tamarind

Tamarind is the sour pulp of an Asian fruit. It is most commonly available compressed into cakes, or refined into tamarind purée, which is sold in jars. Tamarind purée is widely available in Asian food shops. To make tamarind water from compressed tamarind, put 100 g (3½ oz) of tamarind into a bowl and cover with 500 ml (17 fl oz/ 2 cups) of boiling water. Allow to steep for 1 hour, stirring occasionally to break up the fibres, then strain.

tatsoi

Related to bok choy (pak choy), tatsoi is an Asian salad vegetable with small, flavoursome dark green leaves that can be tossed raw through salads, or added briefly to stir-fries.

thai basil

Thai basil is a distinctively flavoured herb with narrower and more deeply coloured leaves than the common basil.

vanilla bean

The long, slim, black vanilla bean has a wonderful caramel aroma that synthetic vanilla can never capture. Good-quality beans are soft and not too dry. Store

unused vanilla pods in a full jar of caster (superfine) sugar, which will not only help to keep the vanilla fresh, but the aroma of the bean will quickly infuse the sugar, making it ideal for use in desserts and baking. See also natural vanilla extract.

vine leaves

The large, green leaves of the grapevine are available packed in tins, jars or plastic packs or in brine. They are used in Greek and Middle Eastern cuisine to wrap foods for cooking. Vine leaves sold in brine should be rinsed before use to remove some of the salty flavour. Fresh, young vine leaves should be simmered in water for 10 minutes, or until soft.

water chestnuts

The white, edible tuber of an aquatic plant, the water chestnut adds a delicate, crunchy texture to many South-East Asian dishes. Fresh water chestnuts can be found in Chinese food stores, and are also sold whole or sliced in tins.

white miso

White miso (which is actually a pale yellow colour) is a fermented paste of soya beans, salt and either rice or barley. It has a sweet, mellow taste and a relatively low salt content. White miso is available from Asian grocery stores and health food stores. See also miso paste.

index

acknowledgements

A heartfelt thanks to Kay Scarlett and Juliet Rogers for allowing me once again to get lost in the world of food and for allowing me my desert island escape..

A huge thank you to Vivien Valk for a beautiful design and book. Thank you for your time and endless enthusiasm. A big thankyou also to Daniela Bertollo for pulling all the pieces together and keeping us on our toes.

Jo Glynn, as always, did a wonderful job testing the recipes and keeping me on track and Katri Hilden kept a sharp editorial eye on my words and wording. Indeed, a big thank you to the whole team at Murdoch Books.

A cookery book has to make you hungry when you look at it and once again Ross Dobson has been the saint in the kitchen. His cooking has turned a recipe into a gorgeous tumble of ingredients and for that he deserves several big hugs and probably a few stiff drinks. Mikkel Vang and Christine Rudolph took the food, added a spoonful of beautiful light, a sprinkle of gorgeous props and a dollop of island magic and created the luscious images that tell this book's story. A big hug for both of you and a very big thank you for all your hard work.

A big thank you also to Anthony Ong for his beautiful shots of Stephanie, Mariana and Letisha. He has given the book its sunny life and perfectly captured the moment when you find yourself on the perfect beach on the perfect day. My thanks also to Katrina Raftery for sprinkling the girls with a little fairy dust and a huge thank-you to Kim Payne for the gorgeous wardrobe and lifestyle styling.

Books have a habit of taking over your life. As always, the biggest thank you goes to the boys in my life. Thank you for forgiving me my occasional absent-minded mothering and for filling the fridge with food you weren't interested in. Apparently not everyone is as excited by chilli prawns and duck salad as I am!

Previously published as Marie Claire Luscious (2005)
Published in 2010 by Murdoch Books
This edition published 2013

Murdoch Books Australia
83 Alexander St
Crows Nest NSW 2065
Phone: +61 (0) 2 8425 0100
Fax: +61 (0) 2 9906 2218
www.murdochbooks.com.au

Publisher: Kay Scarlett
Project manager and editors: Daniela Bertollo, Desney King and Zoe Harpham
Art direction and layout: Vivien Valk
Stylists: Kim Payne (fashion), Christine Rudolph (food) and Michele Cranston (food)
Photographers: Mikkel Vang (food) and Anthony Ong (lifestyle)
Food preparation: Ross Dobson
Models: Stephanie Eales, Letisha Gibara, Mariana from Chic Management
Production: Joan Beal

National Library of Australia Cataloguing-in-Publication Data

Title:	Marie claire summer.
ISBN:	9781742660462 (pbk.)
Notes:	Includes index.
Subjects:	Cookery (Natural foods)
	Quick and easy cookery.
	Nutrition.
	Food.
	Also Titled: Marie Claire (North Sydney, N.S.W.)
Dewey Number:	641.514

A catalogue record for this book is available from the British Library.

Colour separation by Splitting Image Colour Studio, Melbourne, Australia.
Printed by 1010 Printing International Limited, China

PRINTED IN CHINA.

IMPORTANT: Those who might be at risk from the effects of salmonella poisoning (the elderly, pregnant women,
young children and those suffering from immune deficiency diseases) should consult their doctor with any concerns
about eating raw eggs.

CONVERSION GUIDE: You may find cooking times vary depending on the oven you are using. For fan-forced
ovens, as a general rule, set the oven temperature to 20°C (35°F) lower than indicated in the recipe.